How to Pay Off Your Mortgage Early While Building a Real Estate Portfolio

Balancing Mortgage Payoff and Investing for Maximum Long-Term Wealth

By Joseph G. Correa

Copyright & Legal Notice

Published by Live Stronger Faster

First Edition, 2026

Table of Contents

Introduction

For decades, homeownership has been considered one of the most powerful ways to build wealth. Owning a home provides stability, security, tax advantages, and the opportunity to build equity over time. At the same time, real estate investing has created more millionaires than almost any other industry in the world. Rental properties, appreciation, leverage, and long-term cash flow have helped ordinary individuals create extraordinary wealth across generations. Yet many people find themselves trapped between two competing financial goals. On one side, they want to pay off their mortgage early and eliminate debt as quickly as possible. On the other side, they want to invest in additional real estate opportunities that can generate long-term passive income and accelerate wealth creation. The challenge becomes understanding how to balance both strategies intelligently without sacrificing financial flexibility, liquidity, or future opportunities.

Many homeowners assume that paying off their mortgage as fast as possible is always the smartest financial decision. Others believe they should never pay off low-interest debt and instead invest every extra dollar into new properties. The truth is that wealth creation is rarely built through extremes. Instead, it is often created through strategic balance, intelligent leverage, disciplined investing, and long-term planning. This book was designed to help you understand how to combine mortgage payoff strategies with real estate portfolio growth so you can create financial freedom without limiting your future potential.

The reality is that your primary residence can either become a financial anchor that slows your growth or a financial tool that helps launch your real estate empire. Many homeowners spend decades paying off their homes without ever building significant investment assets beyond their primary residence. While they eventually become debt-free, they may reach retirement with limited cash flow, minimal passive income, and very few appreciating assets outside their home equity. On the other hand, some investors become overleveraged, aggressively buying properties while neglecting risk management, liquidity, and debt reduction. When markets shift, interest rates rise, or vacancies occur, their financial position can quickly become unstable. This book focuses on helping you avoid both extremes by creating a strategic system that balances mortgage acceleration with real estate portfolio growth.

One of the most important concepts you will learn throughout this book is that wealth is often built through cash flow, leverage, and time. Real estate allows investors to control large appreciating assets with relatively small amounts of capital through financing. Over time, tenants may help pay down mortgages, property values may appreciate, rents may rise, and tax advantages may improve overall returns. Meanwhile, strategic mortgage payoff methods can reduce financial stress, lower interest costs, and increase monthly cash flow. The goal is not simply to eliminate debt as fast as possible or acquire properties endlessly without structure. The goal is to create a sustainable financial strategy that allows you to increase net worth, improve cash flow, reduce risk, and maintain flexibility over the long term.

Throughout history, some of the wealthiest individuals in the world have understood the power of using debt strategically rather than emotionally. Debt itself is not automatically bad. High-interest consumer debt that finances depreciating assets often destroys wealth. However, properly structured mortgage debt tied to appreciating assets can become a powerful wealth-building tool when managed correctly. Understanding the difference between destructive debt and productive debt is essential. This book will help you learn how to evaluate mortgage decisions not only from an emotional perspective but also from a mathematical, strategic, and long-term wealth-building perspective.

One of the biggest mistakes homeowners make is focusing only on becoming debt-free without considering opportunity cost. Every extra dollar used toward paying down a low-interest mortgage is a dollar that cannot be invested elsewhere. Sometimes paying down debt aggressively makes sense. Other times, using that same capital to purchase a cash-flowing rental property may create significantly greater long-term wealth. The key is understanding how to evaluate interest rates, cash flow, appreciation potential, tax implications, liquidity needs, market conditions, and personal financial goals before making decisions. This book will help you understand when aggressive mortgage payoff may be beneficial and when investing in additional real estate opportunities may create better overall outcomes.

At the same time, many aspiring investors delay entering the real estate market because they feel pressured to fully pay off their primary mortgage first. Years pass while property prices rise, rents increase, and investment opportunities disappear. Meanwhile, inflation slowly reduces purchasing power, and the cost of waiting becomes larger over time. In many situations, a balanced approach may allow individuals to reduce mortgage debt steadily while simultaneously building a rental portfolio that creates passive income and long-term equity growth. Understanding how to create this balance can dramatically accelerate financial freedom.

This book is also designed to help you understand how real estate investing and mortgage payoff strategies evolve throughout different stages of life and financial growth. A young investor with stable income and strong earning potential may prioritize acquiring appreciating assets early while maintaining manageable mortgage debt. A higher-income professional may choose to optimize tax strategies while using leverage strategically to build multiple income-producing properties. A family nearing retirement may prioritize reducing debt aggressively while stabilizing cash flow and protecting accumulated wealth. There is no one-size-fits-all strategy. Your ideal plan depends on your income, goals, risk tolerance, market conditions, age, financial obligations, and desired lifestyle.

One of the most powerful advantages of real estate investing is the ability to create multiple streams of income while simultaneously building long-term equity. Rental properties can generate monthly cash flow that helps cover mortgage payments, living expenses, reinvestment opportunities, and future acquisitions. Over time, properly selected properties may appreciate significantly in value while tenants continue reducing the principal balance through mortgage payments. This combination of appreciation, leverage, amortization, and cash flow creates a wealth-building engine that can dramatically outperform relying solely on paying down a primary mortgage. However, success requires planning, discipline, market awareness, and strong financial management. This book will teach you how to approach these strategies responsibly and intelligently.

You will also learn that liquidity and financial flexibility are critical components of long-term wealth creation. Many homeowners aggressively pay down their mortgages only to discover they have limited cash reserves when investment opportunities appear or unexpected emergencies arise. Being "equity rich" but "cash poor" can create significant financial limitations. Maintaining healthy reserves, preserving access to capital, and protecting financial flexibility often matter just as much as reducing debt balances. Strategic investors understand that access to liquidity allows them to take advantage of opportunities during market shifts, economic downturns, and distressed property situations.

Another important topic explored throughout this book is the psychological side of debt and investing. Money decisions are rarely based solely on mathematics. Emotional comfort, stress levels, family responsibilities, personal values, and risk tolerance all influence financial decisions. Some individuals sleep better knowing their mortgage balance is decreasing rapidly. Others feel more motivated by building passive income streams and investment assets. Neither perspective is

Financial freedom ultimately means having enough assets, income, and flexibility to control your time and your life. For some people, that may mean becoming entirely debt-free while owning several cash-flowing rental properties outright. For others, it may mean maintaining low-interest mortgage debt while generating strong passive income from appreciating assets. The exact path may differ, but the core principles remain the same: disciplined financial management, intelligent leverage, long-term planning, strategic investing, and continuous learning.

The purpose of this book is to help you think differently about mortgages, debt, and wealth creation. Your mortgage does not have to be viewed solely as a burden. When managed correctly, it can become part of a larger financial strategy that supports portfolio growth, cash flow generation, and long-term financial independence. By learning how to balance mortgage payoff with real estate investing, you can potentially create greater financial security, stronger passive income streams, and significantly higher long-term net worth.

As you move through this book, you will discover practical strategies, real-world concepts, financial frameworks, and long-term planning techniques designed to help you build wealth intelligently. You will learn how to evaluate opportunities, reduce unnecessary financial risk, improve cash flow, and make strategic decisions that align with your long-term goals. Whether you are just beginning your financial journey or already own investment properties, this book is designed to help you create a smarter, more balanced approach to mortgage management and real estate wealth creation. The journey toward financial freedom is rarely built through a single decision. It is built through consistent actions, strategic planning, disciplined investing, and the ability to think long term. By combining intelligent mortgage payoff strategies with responsible real estate investing, you can potentially create a financial future that provides security, flexibility, passive income, and lasting wealth for yourself and future generations.

Chapter 1

The Foundation of Wealth – Understanding the Balance Between Mortgage Payoff and Real Estate Investing

One of the most important financial decisions a person will ever make is deciding how to manage their mortgage while building long-term wealth. For many homeowners, the mortgage represents both security and obligation. It provides shelter, stability, and the opportunity to build equity over time, yet it also represents decades of monthly payments, interest expenses, and financial commitment. At the same time, real estate investing has become one of the most powerful wealth-building tools available to ordinary individuals. The challenge for many people is determining whether they should focus primarily on paying off their mortgage early or begin investing in additional real estate opportunities before becoming debt-free. Understanding how to balance these goals is one of the foundational principles of long-term financial success.

For decades, traditional financial advice often centered around aggressively paying off debt as quickly as possible. Many families viewed becoming mortgage-free as the ultimate sign of financial freedom. Eliminating a mortgage payment reduced monthly expenses, lowered stress, and provided emotional security. However, over time, many financially successful investors began recognizing that low-interest mortgage debt tied to appreciating real estate assets could also become a strategic financial tool. Instead of focusing solely on eliminating debt, they learned how to use leverage responsibly to acquire additional assets capable of generating cash flow, appreciation, and long-term wealth.

The key difference between financially productive debt and financially destructive debt lies in what the borrowed money is used to acquire. Consumer debt often finances depreciating items such as vehicles, luxury goods, or lifestyle spending that loses value over time. Mortgage debt, on the other hand, may finance appreciating assets capable of producing long-term income and equity growth. Understanding this distinction is critical because it changes the way successful investors think about debt entirely. The goal is not simply to avoid all debt. The goal is to avoid bad debt while learning how to use productive debt strategically.

One of the first concepts homeowners must understand is opportunity cost. Opportunity cost refers to what you give up when choosing one financial decision over another. For example, imagine a homeowner with an extra $50,000 available. They could use that money to make a large lump-sum payment toward their mortgage, reducing interest costs and accelerating payoff. Alternatively, they could use that same $50,000 as a down payment on a rental property that generates monthly cash flow, appreciates in value, and provides tax advantages. Both choices may improve financial stability, but the long-term financial outcomes could be dramatically different depending on market conditions, cash flow performance, appreciation, and financing structures.

Many people automatically assume paying off their mortgage early is always the safest financial move because it reduces debt obligations. While reducing debt can absolutely improve financial security, it is important to understand that wealth is often created through asset accumulation rather than debt elimination alone. A homeowner who spends thirty years aggressively paying off their mortgage but never invests in additional assets may eventually own their home free and clear, yet still have limited passive income. Another individual who strategically balances mortgage reduction with acquiring income-producing rental properties may reach retirement with multiple streams of income, appreciating assets, and significantly greater net worth.

This does not mean everyone should aggressively leverage themselves into investment properties without caution. In fact, one of the biggest mistakes inexperienced investors make is overextending financially without sufficient reserves, planning, or cash flow analysis. The purpose of this book is not to encourage reckless borrowing. Instead, the goal is to help you understand how to create balance. Financial freedom is often built through a combination of reducing unnecessary liabilities while simultaneously increasing income-producing assets. This balanced approach allows homeowners to strengthen financial stability while still taking advantage of long-term investment opportunities.

Real estate investing offers several unique advantages that make it particularly attractive for long-term wealth creation. First, real estate allows investors to use leverage. Unlike many other investments, real estate investors may control large assets using relatively small down payments. A property worth hundreds of thousands of dollars may be acquired with a fraction of that amount upfront through financing. Over time, appreciation may increase the property's value while tenants help reduce the mortgage balance through rental payments. This combination creates a powerful long-term wealth-building cycle.

Second, rental properties may generate monthly cash flow. Positive cash flow occurs when rental income exceeds mortgage payments, taxes, insurance, maintenance, and operating expenses. This monthly income may then be used to accelerate mortgage payoff on a primary residence, fund additional investments, build reserves, or improve overall financial flexibility. Over time, rising rents may further improve profitability while fixed mortgage payments remain relatively stable.

Third, real estate often provides tax advantages unavailable through many other investments. Depreciation, mortgage interest deductions, business expense deductions, and other tax strategies may improve overall returns while reducing taxable income. Strategic investors understand that long-term wealth is not built solely by earning income but also by managing taxes efficiently. Properly structured real estate investments may create substantial long-term financial benefits when combined with intelligent tax planning.

One of the most misunderstood aspects of mortgage payoff strategies is the emotional relationship many people have with debt. For some homeowners, carrying mortgage debt creates significant psychological stress regardless of interest rate or investment potential. The emotional relief of becoming debt-free provides peace of mind that may outweigh potential investment returns. For others, maintaining low-interest mortgage debt while investing aggressively feels financially empowering because they view leverage as a tool for growth. Neither perspective is inherently wrong. Financial decisions must align not only with mathematical analysis but also with personal comfort levels, family responsibilities, and long-term lifestyle goals.

Another important factor is inflation. Inflation gradually reduces the purchasing power of money over time. Fixed-rate mortgage debt may become easier to repay in future dollars as wages, rental income, and property values rise. This means that a mortgage payment fixed today may feel significantly smaller twenty years later due to inflation and income growth. At the same time, appreciating real estate assets may increase in value while generating higher rental income over time. Investors who understand inflation often recognize that holding low-interest fixed mortgage debt while owning appreciating assets may create long-term financial advantages.

However, market cycles must also be considered carefully. Real estate markets do not move upward forever without interruptions. Property values may fluctuate. Interest rates may rise. Rental demand may change. Economic downturns may affect cash flow and financing availability. This is why risk management remains one of the most important principles in real estate investing. Investors who rely too heavily on debt without maintaining reserves or stable cash flow may struggle during difficult periods. Building wealth responsibly requires preparation, patience, and financial discipline.

Liquidity is another major consideration when balancing mortgage payoff and investing. Many homeowners become "equity rich but cash poor" by placing every available dollar into mortgage reduction. While their equity position improves, they may lack accessible funds for emergencies, opportunities, repairs, or investments. Maintaining liquidity allows investors to adapt during changing market conditions and take advantage of opportunities when they arise. Strong reserves provide stability and reduce the likelihood of financial stress during unexpected events.

The concept of financial flexibility is closely tied to liquidity. Financial flexibility means having options. A homeowner with reserves, manageable debt obligations, and strong cash flow can make strategic decisions more confidently. They may refinance, purchase additional properties, invest during downturns, or adjust financial strategies as circumstances evolve. Flexibility often creates opportunity because it allows individuals to respond strategically rather than emotionally during periods of uncertainty.

One of the most effective long-term wealth-building strategies involves combining mortgage reduction with strategic investing. For example, a homeowner may continue making consistent extra payments toward their mortgage while also saving for rental property acquisitions. Another investor may use rental property cash flow specifically to accelerate mortgage payoff on their primary residence. Others may refinance strategically to lower interest rates, improve cash flow, or access capital for investments while maintaining manageable debt structures. There are many possible approaches depending on financial goals, market conditions, income stability, and risk tolerance.

High-income earners often face unique decisions when balancing mortgage payoff and investing. Individuals with strong incomes may have the ability to aggressively reduce mortgage debt while simultaneously investing heavily in real estate. Tax strategies, business ownership, asset protection planning, and cash flow optimization often become increasingly important at higher income levels. In many cases, preserving liquidity and leveraging tax advantages strategically may create greater long-term financial outcomes than focusing solely on debt elimination.

Age and life stage also influence strategy. Younger investors may prioritize long-term appreciation and portfolio growth because they have more time to recover from market fluctuations and benefit from compounding growth. Families with children may prioritize stability, reserves, and manageable obligations. Individuals nearing retirement may focus more heavily on reducing debt, stabilizing income, and protecting assets. Financial planning must evolve as personal goals and responsibilities change over time.

One of the most powerful wealth-building concepts is understanding how time multiplies financial decisions. Small strategic decisions repeated consistently over decades often create extraordinary results. A single rental property acquired early in life may eventually appreciate significantly while producing decades of rental income and mortgage reduction. Extra mortgage payments made consistently may save tens or hundreds of thousands of dollars in long-term interest. Over time, the compounding effects of appreciation, amortization, rental growth, and disciplined investing can become enormous.

Patience is critical because real estate wealth is rarely built overnight. Many successful investors spent years gradually building portfolios one property at a time while maintaining disciplined financial habits. They focused on cash flow, long-term value, conservative financing, and sustainable growth rather than chasing rapid wealth through speculation.

Consistency often matters more than speed. Sustainable strategies usually outperform aggressive strategies that create excessive financial stress or risk. This chapter serves as the foundation for understanding the relationship between mortgage payoff and real estate investing. Throughout this book, you will learn how to evaluate opportunities strategically, reduce unnecessary financial risk, improve cash flow, and create a personalized plan that aligns with your long-term financial goals. You will discover how to analyze mortgage structures, rental opportunities, refinancing options, cash flow systems, tax strategies, and investment timing more effectively.

Ultimately, financial freedom is not simply about eliminating debt or accumulating properties. It is about creating control over your financial future. It means building a life where your income, investments, and assets provide flexibility, stability, and opportunity. By learning how to balance mortgage payoff with intelligent real estate investing, you may create a powerful long-term strategy capable of producing lasting wealth for yourself and future generations.

The Teacher Who Built Wealth One Property at a Time

When Daniel Ramirez bought his first home at thirty-two years old, he believed he had achieved the American Dream. The small three-bedroom home sat on a quiet street lined with oak trees and aging sidewalks. It was not luxurious, but to Daniel, it represented stability after years of renting small apartments and struggling to save money while working as a high school history teacher. The mortgage payment stretched his budget tightly, yet he felt proud every time he unlocked the front door because he knew he was finally building equity instead of paying rent to a landlord.

For the first few years, Daniel focused entirely on paying down his mortgage as quickly as possible. Every extra dollar from tutoring students, summer school teaching, and coaching baseball went directly toward his principal balance. He skipped vacations, delayed replacing his aging car, and rarely spent money on entertainment. Watching the mortgage balance slowly decrease gave him a sense of accomplishment and security. He dreamed about the day he would become completely debt-free.

One evening, Daniel attended a neighborhood barbecue hosted by his next-door neighbor, Marcus. Unlike Daniel, Marcus seemed financially relaxed despite owning multiple properties. During their conversation, Marcus mentioned that one of his rental homes had just increased in value by nearly $80,000 over the past several years while also generating monthly cash flow. Daniel listened carefully but remained skeptical. To him, debt still represented danger, and owning additional properties sounded stressful and risky.

Over the following months, Daniel became increasingly curious about real estate investing. He started reading books, listening to podcasts, and studying how rental properties worked. What surprised him most was learning how many successful investors used financing strategically rather than avoiding debt entirely. He began realizing that while aggressively paying down his mortgage reduced interest expenses, it also limited his ability to invest in appreciating assets that could generate additional income.

One afternoon, Marcus invited Daniel to visit one of his rental duplexes. The property was modest but well maintained. The tenants paid rent consistently, and Marcus explained how the rental income covered the mortgage, taxes, insurance, maintenance, and still produced monthly profit. Daniel was fascinated by the numbers. For the first time, he saw how a property could function not only as shelter but also as a long-term financial asset.

That night, Daniel reviewed his finances carefully. He had spent years making extra mortgage payments and had accumulated significant equity in his home. However, his savings account remained relatively small because nearly all excess cash had gone toward principal reduction. He realized that although he had reduced his mortgage balance substantially, he had not built additional income streams. If he lost his teaching job or faced a financial emergency, his home equity alone would not easily cover his living expenses. Over the next year, Daniel shifted his strategy carefully. Instead of placing every extra dollar toward mortgage reduction, he began building a dedicated investment savings account. He continued making modest extra mortgage payments but focused more heavily on increasing liquidity and preparing for his first investment property. The process required patience and discipline because he wanted to avoid overextending financially.

Eventually, Daniel found a small duplex located near a growing college campus. The property needed cosmetic improvements but had strong rental demand and positive cash flow potential. Nervous but excited, he used a portion of his savings and some equity from his primary residence to purchase the duplex. The first few months were stressful. Repairs cost more than expected, one tenant moved out unexpectedly, and Daniel questioned whether he had made a mistake.

However, things slowly stabilized. After renovating the vacant unit, Daniel rented it to graduate students who consistently paid on time. Within a year, the duplex generated enough cash flow to cover all expenses while providing additional monthly income. For the first time in his life, Daniel experienced the power of passive income. Even while teaching full-time, his rental property quietly generated cash flow and built equity every month. As Daniel gained confidence, he continued educating himself about real estate, financing, and cash flow management. He learned the importance of maintaining reserves, screening tenants carefully, and evaluating properties conservatively. Instead of rushing to acquire as many properties as possible, he focused on buying stable cash-flowing assets gradually and responsibly.

Several years later, Daniel purchased a second rental property, followed by a small four-unit building. By this point, the combined rental income from his portfolio covered a significant portion of his living expenses. He still had a mortgage on his primary residence, but he no longer viewed it solely as debt. Instead, he understood how to balance debt reduction with asset accumulation strategically.

One of the biggest turning points came during an economic slowdown. Several of Daniel's colleagues panicked about layoffs, rising costs, and financial uncertainty. While Daniel felt concern like everyone else, his rental income provided stability that many others lacked. His tenants continued paying rent, his fixed-rate mortgages remained stable, and his reserves allowed him to navigate uncertainty without panic. For the first time, Daniel fully understood the true meaning of financial flexibility.

Over the following decade, property values appreciated steadily while rental income increased significantly. Daniel refinanced strategically several times to lower interest rates and improve cash flow. He never became reckless or overleveraged because he remembered how difficult financial stress had felt earlier in life. His focus remained on sustainable growth, strong reserves, and long-term wealth creation.

Eventually, the income from Daniel's rental portfolio exceeded his teaching salary. Although he loved teaching and continued working for several more years, he realized he now had options. He was no longer financially trapped by a paycheck. His investments provided freedom, flexibility, and security that he once believed were impossible.

One afternoon, while sitting on the porch of his now nearly paid-off primary residence, Daniel reflected on how dramatically his financial mindset had changed over the years. Early in life, he believed financial success meant eliminating all debt as quickly as possible. Over time, he learned that wealth creation involved balancing debt reduction with strategic investing, cash flow generation, and long-term planning.

By the age of fifty-eight, Daniel owned several cash-flowing properties, had substantial equity, healthy reserves, and a nearly eliminated mortgage balance on his home. More importantly, he had created financial peace of mind without sacrificing opportunity. His investments now generated enough passive income to support his lifestyle comfortably even after retirement. As Daniel watched the sunset from his porch that evening, he realized the greatest lesson was not about becoming rich quickly. It was about building wealth steadily through patience, discipline, and balanced decision-making. He had learned that financial freedom was not created through fear of debt or reckless investing but through understanding how to use money strategically over time.

The journey had not been perfect. There were stressful moments, difficult repairs, market fluctuations, and periods of uncertainty. Yet every challenge taught him valuable lessons about risk management, resilience, and long-term planning. Most importantly, Daniel discovered that his mortgage was never simply a monthly payment. When managed intelligently, it became part of a much larger financial strategy that helped him build lasting wealth and financial independence.

Years later, Daniel often shared his experiences with younger teachers who felt overwhelmed by rising housing costs and financial uncertainty. He encouraged them to think beyond simply paying bills month to month. He taught them to view financial decisions strategically, maintain discipline, and focus on building income-producing assets over time. Many were surprised to hear that the quiet history teacher who once worried constantly about money had eventually built a portfolio capable of transforming his future. Daniel's story became proof that ordinary individuals do not need extraordinary income to build wealth. They need education, patience, discipline, and the willingness to think long term. By balancing mortgage payoff with responsible real estate investing, Daniel gradually created the financial freedom he once believed only wealthy people could achieve.

Chapter 2

Understanding Opportunity Cost – When Paying Off Your Mortgage May Help or Hurt Long-Term Wealth

One of the most important concepts in personal finance and real estate investing is opportunity cost. Although the term may sound technical, opportunity cost affects nearly every financial decision people make throughout their lives. In simple terms, opportunity cost refers to what you potentially give up when choosing one option over another. Every dollar spent, invested, saved, or used to reduce debt carries an alternative possibility. Understanding opportunity cost is critical when deciding whether to aggressively pay off your mortgage early or use your available capital to invest in additional income-producing assets.

For many homeowners, making extra mortgage payments feels like the safest and most responsible financial decision possible. Reducing debt provides emotional comfort, lowers long-term interest expenses, and increases home equity more quickly. Watching a mortgage balance decline can create a powerful sense of progress and financial security. However, every additional dollar placed toward principal reduction is also a dollar that cannot be invested elsewhere. This is where opportunity cost becomes one of the most important factors in long-term wealth creation.

Imagine two homeowners with identical incomes, homes, and financial situations. Both receive a $100,000 inheritance. The first homeowner immediately uses the full amount to reduce their mortgage balance. Their monthly mortgage payment remains the same unless the loan is recast, but their payoff timeline shortens significantly, and they reduce future interest costs. The second homeowner instead uses the $100,000 as down payments on two cash-flowing rental properties. Over time, those properties appreciate in value, tenants reduce the mortgage balances, rents increase, and the properties generate passive income each month. Twenty years later, both individuals may be financially stable, but the second homeowner may potentially possess a significantly higher net worth and substantially greater passive income due to the power of leveraged real estate investing.

This example does not automatically mean investing is always the superior choice. Opportunity cost is not about finding one universal answer that applies to every situation. Instead, it is about understanding the tradeoffs associated with each decision. Sometimes aggressively paying down debt creates the best long-term outcome. In other situations, investing excess capital may create dramatically greater wealth. The key is learning how to evaluate financial decisions strategically rather than emotionally.

One major factor influencing opportunity cost is interest rates. A homeowner with a mortgage interest rate of 2.75 percent may experience a very different opportunity cost calculation than someone carrying a mortgage at 8 percent. Low-interest mortgage debt is often considered relatively inexpensive capital, especially during periods of inflation. If investments can reasonably produce returns significantly higher than the mortgage interest rate over the long term, investing may mathematically outperform aggressive debt reduction. However, if interest rates are high or investment returns are uncertain, reducing debt may become far more attractive.

Inflation also plays a major role in opportunity cost calculations. Inflation gradually reduces the purchasing power of money over time. Fixed-rate mortgage debt becomes easier to repay in future dollars because wages, rents, and property values may rise while the mortgage payment remains relatively stable. Investors who understand inflation recognize that holding low-interest fixed debt while owning appreciating assets may create long-term financial advantages. In many cases, inflation effectively reduces the real cost of mortgage debt over time. At the same time, opportunity cost must also account for risk. Investment returns are never guaranteed. Real estate markets fluctuate, tenants may stop paying rent, maintenance expenses may increase, and economic downturns may reduce property values temporarily. Paying off a mortgage, however, creates a guaranteed return equal to the mortgage interest rate because every dollar paid toward principal reduces future interest expenses. Some homeowners value this certainty more than the possibility of higher but less predictable investment returns.

Another critical factor is liquidity. Liquidity refers to how easily assets can be converted into accessible cash. Many homeowners aggressively pay down mortgage balances only to later realize they have very limited liquid savings available for emergencies, investments, or unexpected opportunities. Home equity may appear substantial on paper, but accessing that equity may require refinancing, obtaining a HELOC, or selling the property. During difficult economic conditions or rising interest rate environments, accessing equity may become more difficult or expensive than expected.

Maintaining liquidity creates flexibility. Investors with strong reserves may take advantage of market opportunities during downturns, purchase discounted assets, or navigate unexpected financial challenges without panic. Opportunity cost analysis should always consider not only potential returns but also the importance of maintaining accessible capital. Financial flexibility often becomes one of the most underrated components of long-term wealth creation.

Tax considerations further complicate opportunity cost decisions. Mortgage interest may provide tax deductions depending on individual financial situations and current tax laws. Real estate investments may offer depreciation benefits, expense deductions, and other tax advantages capable of improving overall returns. In some situations, investing may create superior after-tax financial outcomes compared to aggressively paying down mortgage debt. Understanding tax implications can significantly influence which strategy produces the strongest long-term results.

One of the biggest mistakes people make is focusing exclusively on eliminating debt without considering asset growth. Financial freedom is usually created not only by reducing liabilities but also by increasing income-producing assets. A homeowner who becomes entirely debt-free but lacks sufficient retirement savings, passive income, or appreciating investments may still face financial limitations later in life. Conversely, an investor who aggressively acquires assets while maintaining reasonable debt structures may eventually create substantial passive income and long-term wealth even before fully eliminating mortgage obligations. Cash flow is another essential part of opportunity cost analysis. A rental property capable of generating positive monthly income may create ongoing financial benefits that compound over time. That monthly cash flow may then be reinvested, used to accelerate mortgage payoff, fund additional investments, or improve overall lifestyle flexibility. Over time, rising rents combined with mortgage amortization may dramatically improve profitability. This creates a compounding wealth-building cycle that aggressive mortgage payoff alone may not fully replicate.

However, cash flow investing requires discipline and proper analysis. Not every property produces positive returns. Many inexperienced investors purchase properties based solely on appreciation expectations without carefully evaluating expenses, financing terms, maintenance costs, vacancy risks, or local rental demand. Poor investment decisions may create financial stress rather than financial freedom. Opportunity cost calculations must include realistic assumptions about cash flow, expenses, risk, and long-term sustainability.

Psychology also plays a significant role in opportunity cost decisions. Some people simply sleep better at night knowing their mortgage balance is declining rapidly. Emotional security has real value. Financial decisions should improve overall quality of life rather than create constant stress or anxiety. If aggressive investing causes overwhelming financial pressure or emotional discomfort, the potential returns may not justify the personal cost. Likewise, individuals who become excessively fearful of all debt may miss valuable long-term opportunities capable of improving financial freedom dramatically.

One effective strategy many financially successful individuals use is balance. Instead of placing every available dollar toward mortgage payoff or investing every dollar aggressively into additional properties, they divide resources strategically between debt reduction, investing, reserves, and liquidity. This balanced approach allows homeowners to reduce financial obligations steadily while still participating in long-term asset growth.

For example, a homeowner may decide to make moderate extra principal payments each month while simultaneously saving for investment property acquisitions. Another individual may purchase a rental property first and then use the property's cash flow specifically to accelerate primary mortgage payoff. Others may prioritize maxing out retirement accounts while gradually building real estate investments over time. There are countless possible combinations depending on income, risk tolerance, goals, age, and market conditions.

Timing also matters significantly when evaluating opportunity cost. Real estate markets move in cycles. Interest rates rise and fall. Economic conditions change. Opportunities that exist today may not exist in the future. Delaying investing for decades while waiting to become completely debt-free may cause individuals to miss years of appreciation, cash flow growth, and compounding wealth creation. On the other hand, investing aggressively during overheated markets without sufficient reserves or financial preparation may increase risk unnecessarily.

Age and life stage often influence how opportunity cost should be evaluated. Younger investors generally have more time to recover from market fluctuations and benefit from long-term appreciation. This longer time horizon may justify greater focus on asset accumulation and investment growth. Individuals nearing retirement may prioritize debt reduction, income stability, and lower financial obligations because preserving wealth becomes increasingly important. Financial strategies should evolve over time rather than remain static.

High-income earners frequently face unique opportunity cost decisions because they often possess greater borrowing power, stronger cash flow, and more complex tax considerations. In many cases, high-income professionals may benefit from preserving liquidity and using leveragc strategically while allowing appreciating assets to grow over time. Business owners, self-employed individuals, and investors often evaluate debt differently because they understand how capital can generate additional income when deployed effectively.

One of the most powerful lessons opportunity cost teaches is that money must be viewed strategically rather than emotionally. Every financial decision carries tradeoffs. There is no perfect strategy that eliminates all risk while maximizing all returns simultaneously. Instead, successful wealth builders learn how to evaluate probabilities, manage risk responsibly, preserve flexibility, and align financial decisions with long-term goals.

Ultimately, the goal is not simply to eliminate debt as fast as possible or acquire as many assets as possible. The true objective is creating sustainable long-term financial freedom. Financial freedom means having enough income, assets, liquidity, and flexibility to control your lifestyle without constant financial stress. Opportunity cost analysis helps individuals understand how each financial decision either accelerates or delays that freedom.

Throughout the remainder of this book, you will continue learning how to evaluate mortgage decisions, investment opportunities, refinancing strategies, cash flow systems, and wealth-building structures through a long-term strategic lens. Understanding opportunity cost is one of the foundational principles that allows homeowners and investors to make smarter decisions capable of transforming their financial futures over time.

The Engineer Who Almost Missed His Opportunity

Michael Turner had always believed that eliminating debt was the key to financial success. Raised by parents who survived difficult economic times, he learned early in life that owing money created vulnerability. His father constantly reminded him that "the borrower is always the servant to the lender," and those words shaped Michael's financial mindset for decades.

By the age of thirty-eight, Michael worked as a successful mechanical engineer earning a strong income. He lived in a beautiful suburban home with his wife Lauren and their two young children. Although his career provided financial stability, Michael remained obsessed with one goal above all others: paying off his mortgage as quickly as possible.

Every bonus, tax refund, overtime payment, and side consulting check went directly toward his mortgage principal. Michael tracked his loan balance obsessively on spreadsheets and celebrated every milestone reduction. While many of his coworkers upgraded cars, traveled frequently, or invested aggressively, Michael focused solely on eliminating debt. One afternoon during lunch, Michael overheard two coworkers discussing their rental properties and passive income. One coworker mentioned that his rental home generated enough monthly cash flow to cover nearly half his mortgage payment. Michael listened politely but dismissed the conversation internally. To him, taking on additional debt to buy more properties sounded dangerous and irresponsible.

Over the next several years, Michael continued accelerating his mortgage payoff aggressively. By age forty-three, he had reduced his mortgage balance dramatically and felt proud of his progress. However, despite his growing home equity, he noticed something troubling. His investment accounts remained relatively small, and nearly all his wealth existed inside his primary residence.

Then something unexpected happened. A newer engineer named Ethan joined Michael's company. Ethan was younger, earned less money, and had purchased his first home years after Michael. Yet Ethan seemed financially relaxed and confident in ways Michael found surprising. During casual conversations, Michael learned that Ethan owned three rental properties in addition to his primary residence.

Curious, Michael finally asked how Ethan managed it financially. Ethan explained that instead of aggressively paying down his mortgage, he focused on acquiring cash-flowing rental properties gradually over time. He maintained strong reserves, purchased conservatively, and allowed tenants to pay down the mortgages on his investment properties. Meanwhile, property appreciation and rising rents steadily increased his net worth and passive income.

Michael remained skeptical but intrigued. That evening, he began researching real estate investing seriously for the first time. What shocked him most was discovering how much property values had appreciated in his city over the previous decade. Many of the rental homes Ethan described had nearly doubled in value while generating income the entire time.

For the first time, Michael began confronting a painful realization: while he had successfully reduced his mortgage balance, he may have sacrificed years of potential asset growth by focusing exclusively on debt elimination.

The realization became even more frustrating when Michael examined local property prices. Homes that once sold for $180,000 now sold for over $400,000. Rental demand had surged due to population growth, and cash-flowing properties were increasingly difficult to acquire affordably. Michael suddenly understood opportunity cost in a deeply personal way.

He had not made a "bad" financial decision by paying down debt aggressively. His family remained financially stable, and his home equity position was strong. However, he now realized that every extra dollar directed exclusively toward mortgage payoff represented potential opportunities he never pursued.

Instead of becoming discouraged, Michael decided to educate himself thoroughly before making changes. He studied real estate investing, financing structures, tax advantages, and risk management. Most importantly, he learned that successful investors rarely viewed financial decisions as all-or-nothing choices. Balance mattered.

Michael and Lauren spent months discussing their goals carefully. They agreed they still valued reducing debt, but they also recognized the importance of building income-producing assets and long-term financial flexibility. Together, they developed a new strategy.

Rather than sending every extra dollar toward their mortgage, they began allocating money into multiple categories simultaneously. Part of their surplus income continued reducing mortgage principal, part increased emergency reserves, and part went toward saving for investment opportunities.

Within eighteen months, Michael purchased his first rental property—a small single-family home near a medical center with strong rental demand. The experience initially felt terrifying. Signing another mortgage contradicted years of financial conditioning. Yet after placing reliable tenants and watching the property generate positive cash flow consistently, Michael's perspective slowly began changing.

Over time, the rental income helped cover repairs, increase reserves, and supplement their household finances. More importantly, Michael realized that his money was finally working for him in multiple ways simultaneously. His primary mortgage balance continued declining steadily while his investment property appreciated and generated income.

Several years later, Michael purchased a duplex and eventually another small rental property. He remained conservative, avoided overleveraging, and maintained strong reserves because financial security still mattered deeply to him. However, he no longer viewed all debt as automatically harmful. He learned to distinguish between destructive consumer debt and productive investment debt tied to appreciating assets.

One evening, nearly fifteen years after first overhearing his coworkers discuss real estate investing, Michael sat quietly reviewing his finances. His primary residence was nearly paid off, his rental portfolio generated strong monthly cash flow, and his overall net worth had increased far beyond what he originally imagined possible.

As he reflected on his journey, Michael realized the biggest lesson was not about choosing between paying off debt or investing. The real lesson involved understanding balance and opportunity cost. By focusing exclusively on debt elimination for so many years, he nearly missed opportunities capable of accelerating long-term wealth dramatically.

Fortunately, he eventually learned that financial success was not built solely by avoiding debt. It was built through intelligent decisions, strategic balance, patience, and understanding how money could be deployed to create future opportunities.

Michael smiled as he closed his laptop. He no longer feared mortgages the way he once had. Instead, he finally understood how to use financial tools strategically to create security, flexibility, and long-term freedom for his family.

Chapter 3

Building the Cash Flow Engine – How Rental Income Can Help Pay Off Your Mortgage Faster

One of the most powerful ways to pay off your mortgage early while building a real estate portfolio is to create a cash flow engine. A cash flow engine is a system of income-producing assets that generates money beyond your regular paycheck. For many homeowners, the primary source of income is their job or business. That income covers housing, food, utilities, transportation, insurance, family expenses, savings, and sometimes investments. But when rental income is added to the picture, the financial structure changes. Instead of relying only on earned income to pay down debt and build wealth, the homeowner begins using asset income to accelerate financial progress.

Rental income is powerful because it can work even when you are not actively working. A tenant pays rent each month, and that rent can cover the mortgage, taxes, insurance, maintenance, management, and reserves on the rental property. When the property is purchased correctly, there may be money left over after expenses. That remaining money is positive cash flow. While a few hundred dollars per month may not seem life-changing at first, the long-term effect can be enormous when that cash flow is used intentionally.

Many people think the only way to pay off a mortgage faster is to earn more money, spend less money, or make painful sacrifices. While those methods can work, they are not the only path. A rental property can become an additional financial worker inside your household. It can produce income that helps make extra payments toward your primary mortgage, build emergency reserves, fund repairs, save for another property, or reduce dependence on your paycheck. When one property becomes two, and two become three, the cash flow engine becomes stronger.

The key is understanding that not all rental income should be treated as personal spending money. A disciplined investor does not immediately use every dollar of rental income to upgrade their lifestyle. Instead, they create a system. First, the property must protect itself. This means setting aside money for repairs, vacancies, property taxes, insurance increases, maintenance, and unexpected expenses. After the property is protected, the remaining cash flow can be directed toward a specific financial goal. In this book, one of the main goals is using real estate income to help eliminate mortgage debt faster while still building a growing portfolio.

A simple example can show the power of this strategy. Imagine you own a rental property that produces $400 per month in true positive cash flow after all expenses and reserves. If you apply that $400 per month toward your primary mortgage, that becomes $4,800 per year in extra principal payments. Over ten years, that is $48,000 in extra payments before considering the interest savings created by reducing the mortgage balance faster. If you later add a second rental producing another $400 per month, your extra payment power becomes $800 per month, or $9,600 per year. Over time, your rental portfolio begins helping you reduce personal debt without requiring the same level of sacrifice from your regular income.

This is why rental income can be more powerful than simple budgeting alone. Budgeting helps you control spending, but investing helps you increase income. A homeowner who only cuts expenses may eventually reach a limit. There are only so many expenses that can be reduced before quality of life begins to suffer. But income-producing assets can expand over time. A rental portfolio can grow, rents can increase, mortgages can amortize, and properties can appreciate. This gives the homeowner a long-term wealth-building advantage that goes beyond simply saving money.

However, building a cash flow engine requires discipline and careful property selection. The biggest mistake new investors make is assuming that any rental property is a good investment. A property must be analyzed carefully before purchase. The investor must estimate rent, mortgage payment, property taxes, insurance, repairs, vacancy, management costs, utilities if applicable, HOA dues, and future capital expenses. A property that looks profitable on the surface may lose money once all true expenses are considered. Cash flow must be real, not imaginary.

True cash flow is what remains after responsible reserves are included. If a property produces $300 per month after paying the mortgage, taxes, and insurance but nothing is set aside for repairs or vacancies, the investor may not actually have positive cash flow. One major repair could erase months or even years of profit. Successful investors think beyond the current month. They prepare for the roof, air conditioner, plumbing issue, tenant turnover, appliance replacement, and insurance increase before those expenses happen. This is what separates sustainable investing from risky investing.

Once a property produces reliable cash flow, the next step is deciding how to use it. Some investors use rental income to build reserves until they have six to twelve months of expenses saved for each property. Others use a percentage of cash flow for extra mortgage payments and another percentage for future investments. A balanced strategy may work best. For example, an investor may keep 50 percent of rental cash flow in property reserves, use 25 percent toward the primary mortgage, and save 25 percent toward the next investment property. As reserves grow stronger, more cash flow may be redirected toward mortgage payoff or additional acquisitions.

The beauty of this strategy is that it creates multiple layers of wealth at the same time. While rental income helps pay down your primary mortgage, tenants are also helping pay down the rental property mortgage. At the same time, the rental property may appreciate in value, rents may increase, and your equity may grow. This means one property can potentially help build wealth in several ways at once: cash flow, loan paydown, appreciation, tax benefits, and inflation protection.

Inflation is especially important in real estate. Over time, rents often rise because the cost of housing, labor, materials, insurance, and property ownership increases. If you own a fixed-rate mortgage on a rental property, your principal and interest payment may stay the same while rental income gradually increases. This can widen the gap between income and expenses, improving cash flow over time. That increased cash flow can then be used to pay off your primary mortgage faster, fund future investments, or create greater financial security. A cash flow engine also creates options. If you rely only on your paycheck, your ability to pay down your mortgage faster depends heavily on your job, business, or active income. But if rental income begins covering part of your expenses, your financial life becomes less fragile. If your job income temporarily decreases, rental income may provide support. If an investment opportunity appears, cash flow and reserves may help you act. If you want to retire earlier, rental income may replace part of your employment income. The more income streams you build, the less dependent you become on any single source.

This does not mean rental properties are completely passive or free from challenges. Real estate investing requires management, decision-making, maintenance, and responsibility. Tenants may move out. Repairs may be needed. Markets may soften. Expenses may rise. However, these challenges can be managed with preparation, conservative numbers, good tenant screening, proper insurance, strong reserves, and disciplined systems. The goal is not to avoid every challenge. The goal is to build a system strong enough to handle challenges without destroying your financial plan.

One of the best ways to build a cash flow engine safely is to start small. Many people believe they need to buy multiple properties quickly to become successful. In reality, one well-selected rental property can teach valuable lessons and create meaningful financial progress. The first property helps you understand tenant management, repairs, expenses, financing, leases, and cash flow. Once you understand the process, you can decide whether to expand. Sustainable wealth is usually built by repeating good decisions, not by rushing into large commitments before you are ready.

House hacking can also be a powerful starting point. House hacking occurs when you use your personal residence to generate income. This may include buying a duplex, triplex, or fourplex and living in one unit while renting the others. It may also include renting a room, garage apartment, guesthouse, or separate living space. House hacking can reduce or eliminate your personal housing expense, allowing you to redirect more of your income toward mortgage payoff or future investments. For many beginners, house hacking is one of the most practical bridges between homeownership and real estate investing.

Another strategy is using rental income specifically as a mortgage acceleration tool. Instead of casually spending rental profits, the investor creates a rule: every dollar of net rental income after reserves goes toward the primary mortgage until the mortgage reaches a target balance. This creates discipline and turns passive income into a focused payoff system. Once the primary mortgage is paid off or reduced to a comfortable level, the same rental income can be redirected toward buying more properties, paying off rental mortgages, or building retirement income. The order of operations matters. Before using rental cash flow aggressively for mortgage payoff, an investor should make sure the rental property is financially protected. Reserves should come first. A property without reserves is vulnerable. If the air conditioning system fails, the roof leaks, or a tenant stops paying, the investor may be forced to use personal savings or credit cards. This can undo progress quickly. Strong reserves allow rental income to remain a tool for wealth instead of becoming a source of stress.

Cash flow should also be evaluated after taxes. Rental income may come with tax advantages, but taxes still matter. Depreciation, interest, repairs, property management, insurance, and other expenses may reduce taxable income, but every investor's situation is different. Working with a qualified tax professional can help you understand how rental income affects your overall tax plan. The goal is not just to earn cash flow but to keep and use that cash flow efficiently.

A rental cash flow engine can also help reduce fear around mortgage debt. Many people feel trapped by their mortgage because the payment depends entirely on their active income. When rental income begins covering part of that payment, the mortgage feels less overwhelming. The homeowner is no longer fighting the debt alone. Their assets are helping them. This shift can be extremely empowering because it changes the emotional experience of debt management. However, it is important to avoid using projected appreciation as a substitute for cash flow. Appreciation is powerful, but it is not guaranteed in the short term. A property that loses money every month may become stressful even if it appreciates over time. Cash flow provides staying power. It allows you to hold properties through market cycles, cover expenses, and avoid forced selling. Investors who prioritize cash flow are often better positioned to survive downturns and benefit from long-term appreciation.

Another important principle is reinvestment. In the early years, rental cash flow may feel small, but reinvested cash flow can create momentum. Cash flow can help fund improvements that increase rent. It can help build reserves for another down payment. It can help reduce high-interest debt. It can help make extra principal payments. When cash flow is reinvested wisely, it becomes seed money for future growth. Over time, small monthly amounts can lead to large financial outcomes.

The ultimate goal is to create a financial system where your assets support your liabilities and eventually replace your active income. Your primary mortgage may begin as your largest monthly expense. But as rental income grows, that expense can become easier to manage. Eventually, the cash flow from your portfolio may cover your mortgage entirely. Later, it may cover your living expenses. Eventually, it may give you the option to work less, retire earlier, travel more, help family, or pursue meaningful projects without depending entirely on a paycheck.

This is why building a cash flow engine is such an important part of paying off your mortgage early while building a real estate portfolio. It allows you to combine two powerful goals instead of choosing only one. You can reduce debt while acquiring assets. You can build equity while creating income. You can improve financial security while expanding long-term opportunity. Instead of viewing mortgage payoff and investing as opposing strategies, rental income allows them to work together.

The key is discipline. Cash flow must be measured honestly, protected with reserves, and directed intentionally. Without discipline, rental income can disappear into lifestyle spending and fail to create long-term progress. With discipline, even modest cash flow can become a powerful wealth accelerator. Every rental payment received from a tenant can become part of a larger financial plan. Every month, your portfolio can help move you closer to debt freedom and financial independence.

As you continue through this book, remember that wealth is often built by creating systems that repeat. A single extra payment helps. A single rental check helps. A single property helps. But the real power appears when those actions become consistent and connected. Rental income creates the engine. Discipline provides the steering wheel. Your mortgage payoff plan provides the destination. When all three work together, you begin building a financial machine that can support you for years, decades, and even future generations.

The Duplex That Paid Down the Dream Home

When Alicia Morgan and her husband, Brian, bought their dream home, they felt both excited and terrified. The house was everything they had hoped for: four bedrooms, a small office, a spacious kitchen, and a backyard where their children could play safely. It was located in a quiet neighborhood with good schools and tree-lined streets. But the mortgage payment was much higher than anything they had paid before, and Alicia often felt nervous when she looked at their monthly budget.

Brian worked in information technology, and Alicia worked as a physical therapist. Together, they earned a solid income, but between the mortgage, childcare, food, car payments, insurance, utilities, and student loans, they did not feel wealthy. They felt busy, responsible, and stretched. Every month, they promised themselves they would make extra payments toward the mortgage, but something always came up. A medical bill, a car repair, a school expense, or a family trip would absorb the extra money before it reached the loan balance. Alicia had always dreamed of paying off their home early. Her parents had paid off their mortgage before retirement, and she remembered how proud they felt. She wanted that same sense of peace. Brian agreed, but he also believed they needed to invest more aggressively if they wanted long-term freedom. They often discussed the same question at the kitchen table after the children went to sleep. Should they put every extra dollar toward the mortgage, or should they try to buy an investment property?

For a long time, fear kept them from acting. Alicia worried about tenants, repairs, and taking on more debt. Brian worried that if they waited too long, real estate prices would keep rising and they would miss their chance. They both wanted financial freedom, but they had different ideas about how to reach it. Alicia wanted safety. Brian wanted growth. Neither was wrong. They simply needed a plan that gave them both.

One Saturday afternoon, Brian showed Alicia a duplex listed for sale twenty minutes from their home. It was not beautiful. The paint was faded, the landscaping was neglected, and the kitchens needed updating. But both units were rentable, the neighborhood was improving, and the numbers appeared promising. Alicia was hesitant, but she agreed to tour it.

Walking through the duplex, Alicia noticed every problem immediately. The floors were scratched. The bathrooms looked old. One air conditioner seemed close to the end of its life. She imagined late-night repair calls and difficult tenants. Brian saw the same problems, but he also saw potential. He saw two rental checks, long-term appreciation, and a property that could eventually help pay off their dream home.

Instead of making an emotional decision, they spent the next two weeks analyzing the numbers carefully. They estimated rent, mortgage payments, taxes, insurance, repairs, vacancy, and reserves. They spoke with a property manager, a contractor, and a lender. They built conservative estimates and promised each other they would not buy unless the property could protect itself financially.

The final numbers showed that after all expenses and reserves, the duplex could produce approximately $500 per month in positive cash flow. It was not enough to make them rich overnight, but it was enough to create momentum. Brian suggested that they use the cash flow specifically for extra payments toward their primary mortgage. Alicia liked that idea because it made the investment feel connected to her goal of debt freedom.

They bought the duplex with a mixture of savings and a carefully structured loan. The first few months were not easy. One unit needed repairs before the new tenant moved in. The property insurance premium was higher than expected. Alicia questioned whether they had made a mistake. But they had built reserves, so the expenses did not create panic. They reminded themselves that real estate investing required patience.

After the repairs were completed, both units were rented to stable tenants. The first month that the duplex produced positive cash flow felt almost magical. Alicia logged into their bank account and saw the rent deposits arrive. After paying the property expenses and setting aside reserves, they had money left over. For the first time, an asset outside their jobs was helping them financially.

True to their plan, they sent the extra cash flow toward their primary mortgage principal. It was only $500, but Alicia felt something shift inside her. The extra payment did not come from sacrifice. It did not come from skipping family activities or working overtime. It came from an asset they owned. Their duplex was helping pay down their dream home.

Month after month, the system continued. Some months were smooth. Other months required repairs or extra reserves. But over the course of the year, the duplex helped them send thousands of extra dollars toward their mortgage. Alicia began to understand what Brian meant by building a cash flow engine. The duplex was not just an investment. It was a financial partner. Two years later, rents in the area increased. After renewing leases and improving one unit, the duplex began producing closer to $750 per month in positive cash flow after reserves. Alicia and Brian increased the amount they sent toward their primary mortgage. They also began saving part of the cash flow for another investment property. Their financial conversations changed from anxiety to strategy.

Alicia still valued mortgage freedom deeply, but she no longer believed the only path was using their paychecks. Brian still wanted portfolio growth, but he now respected the importance of reserves, stability, and debt reduction. The duplex had taught them how to combine both goals. They were paying down their home faster while also building long-term wealth through real estate.

Five years after buying the duplex, Alicia reviewed their mortgage statement and realized they had reduced their primary mortgage balance far more than expected. The extra payments from rental cash flow had shortened their projected payoff timeline significantly. At the same time, the duplex had appreciated in value, and its mortgage balance had decreased because the tenants had been paying rent every month.

The realization amazed her. They had not chosen between paying off their mortgage and investing. They had used investing to help pay off their mortgage. The strategy had not been perfect or effortless, but it had worked. Their net worth had grown, their cash flow had improved, and their confidence had increased.

Eventually, Alicia and Brian purchased a second rental property, this time with even more knowledge and discipline. They kept the same rule: protect the property first, maintain reserves, and use a portion of cash flow to accelerate the mortgage on their primary home. Their children grew up watching their parents discuss assets, debt, discipline, and long-term planning at the dinner table. Money became less mysterious and less frightening.

Years later, Alicia stood in the backyard of their dream home watching her children play. The same home that once made her nervous now felt like a symbol of possibility. The mortgage balance was much lower, their rental portfolio was stronger, and their financial future felt more secure. She smiled as she thought about the old duplex with faded paint and scratched floors. At first, she had only seen problems. Now she saw the beginning of their freedom.

The duplex had not made them wealthy overnight. It had done something better. It had taught them how money could be organized, directed, and multiplied. It had shown them that rental income could become a bridge between debt freedom and wealth creation. Most of all, it had taught Alicia and Brian that financial freedom did not require choosing between safety and growth. With the right plan, the right discipline, and the right cash flow engine, they could build both.

Chapter 4

Leveraging Equity Wisely — Using Home Equity to Build Wealth Without Becoming Overleveraged

Home equity is one of the most valuable financial resources many homeowners possess, yet very few people fully understand how to use it strategically. Equity is created when the value of a property exceeds the remaining balance owed on the mortgage. As homeowners make monthly payments and properties appreciate over time, equity gradually grows. For some homeowners, equity simply represents security and ownership. For others, it becomes a powerful financial tool capable of accelerating wealth creation, increasing cash flow, funding investments, and creating long-term financial flexibility.

The challenge is learning how to use home equity wisely rather than emotionally. Many homeowners either avoid using their equity completely or misuse it in ways that weaken their long-term financial future. Some people leave large amounts of equity untouched for decades while struggling with cash flow or missing investment opportunities. Others aggressively borrow against every dollar available and create excessive debt obligations that become difficult to manage during economic downturns or rising interest rate environments. The goal is not to avoid leverage completely or use it recklessly. The goal is to understand how leverage works and apply it carefully as part of a larger wealth-building strategy.

Leverage is one of the most powerful concepts in real estate investing. In simple terms, leverage means using borrowed money to control larger assets. Real estate allows investors to acquire appreciating properties with relatively small amounts of upfront capital compared to the total property value. A person may control a $400,000 property with a much smaller down payment while benefiting from appreciation on the entire asset. This ability to use financing strategically is one of the reasons real estate has created substantial wealth for so many investors over long periods of time.

However, leverage magnifies both opportunity and risk. When property values rise and rental income remains stable, leverage may accelerate wealth creation dramatically. But when markets decline or income becomes unstable, excessive leverage may create serious financial pressure. This is why using equity wisely requires discipline, conservative planning, strong reserves, and realistic expectations. One of the most common ways homeowners access equity is through a home equity line of credit, commonly known as a HELOC. A HELOC allows homeowners to borrow against the available equity in their property while usually paying interest only on the amount used. Unlike a standard mortgage that distributes a fixed lump sum, a HELOC works more like a revolving credit line. Investors often use HELOCs to fund down payments, renovations, emergency reserves, short-term financing, or investment opportunities.

Another popular strategy is a cash-out refinance. In a cash-out refinance, the homeowner replaces their existing mortgage with a larger loan and receives the difference in cash. During periods of low interest rates, many homeowners used cash-out refinances to reduce monthly payments, access investment capital, or restructure debt. However, refinancing also increases debt obligations and may extend repayment timelines, so it must be evaluated carefully.

One of the most important principles when using home equity is understanding the difference between productive debt and destructive debt. Productive debt is used to acquire assets that may appreciate, generate income, or improve long-term financial positioning. Destructive debt is typically used to finance depreciating items or temporary lifestyle upgrades that produce no future income. For example, using home equity to purchase a cash-flowing rental property may create future monthly income, appreciation, tax benefits, and long-term equity growth. Using home equity to purchase luxury vehicles, expensive vacations, or high-end consumer goods often weakens long-term financial stability because those items lose value while the debt remains. The same equity tool can either build wealth or destroy financial flexibility depending on how it is used.

One of the biggest mistakes homeowners make is assuming that because they have large amounts of equity, they are automatically financially secure. Equity alone does not pay monthly bills. A homeowner may have hundreds of thousands of dollars in equity yet struggle financially if cash flow is weak or reserves are limited. Real financial strength comes from combining equity with liquidity, income stability, reserves, and manageable debt obligations.

Liquidity becomes especially important during difficult economic periods. Investors who extract too much equity without maintaining reserves may become vulnerable to vacancies, repairs, job loss, medical emergencies, or rising interest rates. During economic downturns, access to financing may tighten unexpectedly. A person who once believed they could always refinance or access more equity may suddenly discover lenders are no longer offering favorable terms. Strong reserves protect against these situations and provide flexibility during uncertainty. Cash flow should remain one of the primary factors when evaluating whether to use equity for investment purposes. A property purchased using leverage should ideally produce reliable positive cash flow after accounting for mortgage payments, taxes, insurance, maintenance, vacancy, property management, and reserves. Appreciation is valuable, but appreciation alone should rarely justify excessive leverage. Cash flow provides stability and allows investors to hold properties during difficult periods rather than being forced to sell under pressure.

Many inexperienced investors become overleveraged because they assume appreciation will continue indefinitely. During strong markets, rapidly increasing property values can create a false sense of financial confidence. Investors may repeatedly refinance properties, extract equity aggressively, and continue purchasing additional assets without maintaining proper reserves. When markets eventually slow or financing conditions change, these investors may struggle because their debt obligations remain fixed while their financial flexibility disappears.

Conservative leverage often produces more sustainable long-term wealth than aggressive speculation. Investors who focus on manageable debt, strong cash flow, adequate reserves, and stable financing structures are usually better positioned to survive economic cycles. Wealth is often built slowly through consistent decisions repeated over time rather than rapid expansion fueled by excessive debt.

Loan-to-value ratio, commonly called LTV, is one of the most important measurements when evaluating leverage risk. LTV compares the amount borrowed against the value of the property. Lower LTV ratios generally provide more financial protection because the homeowner maintains a larger equity cushion. Higher LTV ratios increase risk because even modest property value declines may significantly reduce available equity or create refinancing difficulties.

Interest rate risk must also be considered carefully. Adjustable-rate debt such as HELOCs may become more expensive when interest rates rise. Investors using variable-rate financing should evaluate whether projected cash flow remains sustainable under higher payment scenarios. Conservative planning involves stress testing investments under different market conditions rather than assuming current conditions will remain unchanged forever.

One of the safest ways to begin using home equity strategically is gradually. Instead of extracting the maximum possible amount immediately, many successful investors start with one carefully selected property and focus on stabilizing it first. They learn how financing works, understand property management responsibilities, build reserves, and evaluate real cash flow performance before expanding further. This gradual approach reduces unnecessary risk while increasing experience and confidence.

House hacking can also be an effective entry point for leveraging equity responsibly. House hacking involves generating rental income from a primary residence by renting rooms, separate units, guest houses, or purchasing small multifamily properties while living in one unit. This strategy allows homeowners to reduce personal housing expenses while building experience and cash flow gradually.

Another important principle is avoiding emotional borrowing decisions. Rising property values often tempt homeowners to view equity as "free money." In reality, every dollar borrowed must eventually be repaid with interest. Investors should evaluate whether borrowed funds are likely to improve long-term financial positioning rather than simply creating temporary lifestyle upgrades.

Inflation also plays an important role in leverage decisions. Fixed-rate mortgage debt may effectively become less expensive over time because wages, rents, and property values may rise while the mortgage payment remains stable. Investors who own appreciating assets financed with long-term fixed-rate debt may benefit significantly during inflationary environments. However, inflation can also increase maintenance costs, insurance premiums, taxes, and interest rates, making conservative planning even more important.

Tax considerations may further influence leverage strategies. Mortgage interest, depreciation, and investment-related expenses may create tax advantages depending on individual circumstances and current laws. However, tax benefits should never become the primary reason for taking on debt. Investments should remain fundamentally sound before considering secondary tax benefits.

One of the greatest long-term advantages of leveraging equity wisely is the ability to accelerate asset accumulation. Instead of waiting decades to save large amounts of cash, investors may acquire appreciating and income-producing assets earlier in life. Time is incredibly powerful because appreciation, rental growth, amortization, and inflation compound over decades. Acquiring assets earlier may create significantly larger long-term outcomes than delaying investments for many years while focusing solely on debt elimination.

Still, the goal should never be growth at all costs. Financial sustainability matters far more than appearing wealthy temporarily. Investors who survive downturns and maintain strong financial foundations are usually positioned to benefit most over the long term. Real estate wealth is often built by people who remain patient, disciplined, and financially flexible during changing market conditions.

Home equity should ultimately be viewed as a strategic tool rather than a source of emotional comfort or impulsive spending power. Used wisely, equity may help create cash flow, acquire appreciating assets, improve long-term financial positioning, and accelerate wealth creation. Used carelessly, it may increase stress, reduce flexibility, and create financial instability.

The key is balance. Strong investors understand that leverage must be combined with cash flow, reserves, conservative planning, and risk management. They focus on building systems rather than chasing short-term excitement. They recognize that wealth is usually created through discipline and consistency rather than rapid speculation.

As you continue through this book, remember that your home equity represents potential. Whether that potential strengthens or weakens your future depends entirely on how wisely you use it. Leverage can become a powerful wealth-building ally when combined with patience, education, cash flow, and responsible financial management.

Using Home Equity to Buy a Rental Property While Accelerating Mortgage Payoff

Let's look at a realistic example of how a homeowner may use equity strategically to build wealth while still reducing mortgage debt over time.

Primary Residence Situation

Home Value: $600,000 Current Mortgage Balance: $300,000 Available Equity: $300,000

The homeowner decides to use a HELOC to access $100,000 of their available equity instead of letting the equity remain inactive.

HELOC Terms

HELOC Amount Used: $100,000 Interest Rate: 8% Interest-Only Payment: Approximately $667/month

The homeowner uses this $100,000 as the down payment and closing costs on a rental property.

Rental Property Purchase

Rental Property Price: $400,000 Down Payment from HELOC: $100,000 New Rental Mortgage: $300,000

Rental Mortgage Terms

Interest Rate: 6.5% 30-Year Fixed Mortgage

Principal & Interest Payment: Approximately $1,896/month

Monthly Rental Expenses

Mortgage Payment: $1,896 Property Taxes: $400 Insurance: $150 Maintenance Reserve: $250 Vacancy Reserve: $150 Property Management: $200

Total Monthly Expenses: $3,046/month

Rental Income

Monthly Rent: $3,700/month

Monthly Cash Flow Calculation

Rental Income: $3,700 Minus Total Expenses: -$3,046

Positive Cash Flow: $654/month

Important Long-Term Wealth Components

Although the monthly cash flow is approximately $654, the property is also building wealth in additional ways.

1. Mortgage Paydown by Tenant

In the first year, approximately $4,000 to $5,000 of the rental mortgage principal may be paid down through tenant rent payments.

2. Property Appreciation

If the property appreciates at an average of 4% annually:

$400,000 × 4% = $16,000 appreciation in year one.

3. Rental Income Growth

If rents increase just 3% annually, the property cash flow may improve significantly over time while the fixed mortgage payment stays relatively stable.

Using Cash Flow to Accelerate Primary Mortgage Payoff

The homeowner decides to apply the $654 monthly cash flow directly toward their primary residence mortgage principal.

Annual Extra Mortgage Payments

$654 × 12 = $7,848/year

If continued consistently, this strategy may remove years from the primary mortgage payoff timeline while the investor simultaneously builds wealth through:

- Rental appreciation
- Tenant mortgage paydown
- Cash flow growth
- Tax advantages
- Equity growth on both properties

Ten-Year Projection Example

Estimated Rental Property Appreciation

$400,000 growing at 4% annually for 10 years:

Approximately $592,000 property value after 10 years.

Estimated Mortgage Balance Reduction

Original Rental Loan: $300,000 Estimated Remaining Balance After 10 Years: Approximately $253,000

Estimated Equity After 10 Years

Property Value: $592,000 Remaining Mortgage: -$253,000

Estimated Equity: Approximately $339,000

Additional Primary Mortgage Reduction

Using the $654 monthly rental cash flow toward the primary mortgage over 10 years:

$654 × 120 months = $78,480 extra principal payments

This does not include the additional interest savings from accelerating the mortgage payoff.

Combined Wealth Effect

After 10 years, the homeowner may potentially achieve:

- Significant reduction in primary mortgage balance
- Over $300,000 in rental property equity
- Increasing rental cash flow
- Additional tax benefits
- Greater financial flexibility
- Multiple appreciating assets

This example demonstrates how equity can become a productive financial tool when combined with disciplined investing, cash flow analysis, reserves, and long-term planning rather than emotional spending or excessive leverage.

Chapter 5

Creating the Long-Term Wealth Blueprint — Balancing Mortgage Freedom, Cash Flow, and Portfolio Growth

One of the greatest financial challenges homeowners face is determining how to balance short-term financial security with long-term wealth creation. Many people spend years focusing entirely on paying bills, reducing debt, and surviving financially month to month without ever developing a clear long-term strategy. Others become so focused on investing aggressively that they neglect stability, liquidity, and financial protection. True financial freedom is rarely created through extremes. Instead, it is often built through a carefully balanced blueprint that combines mortgage reduction, cash flow generation, asset accumulation, risk management, and long-term planning.

A long-term wealth blueprint is not simply a financial goal. It is a complete system designed to organize how income, assets, debt, cash flow, reserves, and investments work together over time. Without a clear blueprint, financial decisions often become reactive and emotional. People may refinance impulsively, invest without strategy, overpay debt at the wrong times, or miss opportunities because they lack direction. A strong blueprint creates clarity and allows homeowners and investors to make decisions intentionally instead of emotionally.

One of the first principles in building a wealth blueprint is understanding that financial freedom means different things to different people. For some individuals, financial freedom means becoming completely debt-free as quickly as possible. For others, it means owning multiple income-producing assets capable of replacing employment income. Some people prioritize flexibility and time freedom, while others focus on building generational wealth for their families. Before creating any financial strategy, it is important to define what success personally means to you.

For example, one person may feel happiest owning a fully paid-off home with minimal financial obligations and moderate retirement savings. Another individual may prefer maintaining low-interest mortgage debt while owning several cash-flowing rental properties producing substantial passive income. Neither approach is automatically right or wrong. The ideal financial blueprint depends on personal goals, risk tolerance, income stability, age, lifestyle preferences, and long-term priorities. One of the most common mistakes homeowners make is focusing exclusively on debt elimination without simultaneously building income-producing assets. While becoming debt-free can absolutely improve financial security, debt reduction alone does not automatically create financial independence. A homeowner may eventually own their property free and clear but still rely heavily on employment income if they lack additional investments or passive income streams.

On the other hand, some investors become obsessed with rapid portfolio expansion while ignoring financial stability. They accumulate large amounts of debt, rely on aggressive appreciation assumptions, and maintain little liquidity. During strong markets, these investors may appear successful. However, during economic downturns, vacancies, or rising interest rate periods, overleveraged investors often experience significant financial stress. Sustainable wealth is usually built through balance rather than extremes.

This is why a long-term wealth blueprint must combine several key components simultaneously. These components often include mortgage management, investment growth, cash flow generation, reserves, tax planning, liquidity, and risk management. The goal is not simply to grow wealth rapidly. The goal is to create a financial structure capable of surviving economic cycles while steadily improving long-term freedom and flexibility. Mortgage management becomes one of the foundational parts of the blueprint because housing often represents the largest expense for most families. How a homeowner manages their mortgage can significantly affect long-term cash flow, investment opportunities, and financial flexibility. Some individuals may benefit from aggressive mortgage payoff strategies, especially if they prioritize emotional security or expect lower future income during retirement. Others may benefit more from preserving liquidity and investing excess capital into appreciating assets producing higher long-term returns.

The key is understanding how each mortgage decision affects the larger financial system. For example, making large extra mortgage payments may reduce long-term interest costs and improve future cash flow once the mortgage is eliminated. However, those same funds could potentially be used for investments capable of generating rental income, appreciation, and tax benefits. A strong financial blueprint evaluates both the immediate and long-term consequences of each choice.

Cash flow is another essential pillar of long-term wealth building. Cash flow provides financial flexibility, stability, and opportunity. A person with strong monthly cash flow often experiences less financial stress because income consistently exceeds expenses. Positive cash flow allows individuals to invest, save, pay down debt, build reserves, and handle unexpected events more comfortably.

Rental properties often become powerful cash flow generators when purchased carefully. Over time, rental income may increase while fixed-rate mortgage payments remain relatively stable. This creates expanding cash flow margins capable of accelerating wealth creation significantly. Rental income may help cover personal living expenses, reduce dependence on employment income, fund retirement accounts, accelerate mortgage payoff, or finance additional investments.

One of the most important lessons successful investors learn is that cash flow provides staying power. Appreciation is valuable, but appreciation alone does not pay bills during difficult periods. Cash flow allows investors to survive downturns, hold properties longer, and avoid panic-driven decisions. Investors who prioritize cash flow are often better positioned to benefit from long-term appreciation because they can maintain ownership during temporary market declines.

Liquidity also plays a critical role in any long-term wealth blueprint. Liquidity refers to accessible cash or assets easily converted into cash. Many homeowners become "equity rich but cash poor" because nearly all their wealth remains trapped inside properties. While equity creates net worth, liquidity creates flexibility. Strong liquidity allows investors to handle repairs, vacancies, economic downturns, medical emergencies, or investment opportunities without relying heavily on new debt.

Emergency reserves are especially important. Many financially successful investors maintain six to twelve months of living expenses and separate property reserves for each rental property they own. These reserves protect against unexpected disruptions and reduce the likelihood of financial panic during difficult situations. Reserves create emotional confidence as well as financial stability.

Another major component of the wealth blueprint involves portfolio growth strategy. Some investors focus on acquiring properties steadily over long periods. Others prioritize paying off existing properties before expanding further. Some individuals prefer single-family rentals, while others focus on multifamily properties, short-term rentals, or mixed-use investments. The correct approach depends on the investor's goals, skills, market knowledge, financing access, and desired lifestyle.

Time horizon also matters significantly. Younger investors may prioritize long-term appreciation and portfolio expansion because they have decades available for compounding growth. Individuals closer to retirement may focus more heavily on reducing debt obligations, stabilizing cash flow, and preserving capital. A financial blueprint should evolve throughout different stages of life rather than remaining fixed forever.

Inflation is another important factor many homeowners overlook. Inflation gradually reduces the purchasing power of money over time while often increasing property values and rental income. Fixed-rate mortgage debt may effectively become easier to repay in future dollars as wages and rents rise. Investors who understand inflation recognize that properly structured real estate assets financed with long-term fixed-rate debt may create substantial long-term advantages.

Tax strategy should also be integrated into the long-term wealth blueprint. Real estate often provides unique tax benefits including depreciation, mortgage interest deductions, expense write-offs, and potential capital gains advantages. Business ownership, retirement planning, and investment structures may further affect overall tax efficiency. Strategic tax planning may significantly improve long-term wealth accumulation when combined with responsible investing.

Risk management remains one of the most important elements of any successful financial system. Risk cannot be eliminated completely, but it can be managed intelligently. Investors reduce unnecessary risk through proper insurance, conservative financing, strong reserves, diversified income sources, careful tenant screening, stable cash flow analysis, and long-term planning. Sustainable investors focus heavily on protecting downside risk while still allowing room for growth.

One common mistake people make is comparing themselves constantly to others. Social media, investment groups, and financial conversations often create pressure to grow faster, buy more properties, or pursue aggressive strategies. However, financial success is highly personal. A strategy that works well for one investor may be completely inappropriate for another. A strong wealth blueprint should align with your own goals, lifestyle, stress tolerance, and long-term priorities rather than external comparisons.

Patience becomes extremely important because wealth creation usually happens gradually. Most financially successful real estate investors did not become wealthy overnight. They often spent years or decades acquiring properties carefully, improving cash flow steadily, managing debt responsibly, and reinvesting profits consistently. Compounding growth may appear slow initially but becomes incredibly powerful over long periods.

Discipline is equally important. Many investors fail not because their strategy was fundamentally flawed but because they became impatient, emotional, or inconsistent. Long-term wealth building requires repeating sound financial decisions consistently even when short-term market conditions create fear or excitement. Sustainable wealth is often built through boring consistency rather than dramatic speculation.

A strong wealth blueprint should also include clear milestones and goals. For example, a homeowner may create a ten-year plan involving reducing their primary mortgage balance by 50 percent while acquiring two cash-flowing rental properties and building one year of reserves. Another individual may focus on replacing 25 percent of employment income with rental cash flow before pursuing more aggressive expansion. Clear goals help create direction and accountability.

Technology and automation may also support the blueprint. Automatic transfers into reserve accounts, investment accounts, retirement plans, and mortgage principal payments help create consistency. Budget tracking software, property management systems, and financial dashboards may improve organization and decision-making quality. Systems reduce emotional decision-making and create stronger long-term habits.

One of the most powerful aspects of real estate wealth building is that multiple wealth-building forces may operate simultaneously. A property may appreciate while tenants reduce the mortgage balance through rent payments. Rental income may increase over time while tax benefits improve overall returns. Meanwhile, extra cash flow may help accelerate mortgage payoff on the primary residence or fund additional investments. This layered wealth-building effect can create extraordinary long-term outcomes when managed responsibly.

Ultimately, the purpose of the wealth blueprint is not simply accumulating money. The true purpose is creating freedom, flexibility, stability, and opportunity. Financial freedom means having options. It means reducing dependence on any single paycheck, improving control over your time, protecting your family, and creating a future aligned with your values and goals.

The blueprint will look different for every individual, but the underlying principles remain consistent: manage debt wisely, build cash flow, maintain reserves, invest strategically, protect liquidity, think long term, and remain disciplined. Over time, these principles work together to create a financial structure capable of supporting lasting wealth and independence.

As you continue through this book, remember that every financial decision becomes part of a larger system. Your mortgage, investments, reserves, income, and cash flow are not isolated pieces. They are connected components of your overall financial life. When organized intentionally, they may work together to accelerate wealth creation while reducing long-term financial stress.

The goal is not perfection. The goal is progress. Small strategic decisions repeated consistently over time often create extraordinary results. A strong wealth blueprint simply provides the roadmap that helps turn those decisions into lasting financial freedom.

Balancing Mortgage Payoff and Rental Property Growth Over 15 Years

Let's examine a realistic example of how a homeowner may combine mortgage reduction, rental property investing, and cash flow growth into a long-term wealth blueprint.

They didn't start this decision thinking in terms of "mortgage payoff speed." They started by asking a more strategic question: *"Do we want financial security faster, or do we want a system that builds income-producing assets over time?"* With a $550,000 home, a $400,000 mortgage at 5.5%, and about $2,000 per month in surplus cash flow, they had enough financial strength to take two very different paths.

In Strategy A, the homeowner focuses entirely on eliminating the mortgage as fast as possible. They apply the full $2,000 monthly surplus toward principal, adding $24,000 per year in extra payments. This reduces the mortgage payoff timeline from 30 years to about 12–13 years. By year 15, the home is fully paid off, and with 4% annual appreciation, it grows to roughly $990,000 in value, creating strong equity and complete debt freedom.

In Strategy B, the homeowner takes a more balanced wealth-building approach. Instead of putting all surplus money into the mortgage, they split it—$1,000 per month toward extra mortgage payments and $1,000 per month toward saving for rental property investments. This slows mortgage payoff slightly to about 17–18 years, but it opens the door to building income-producing assets much earlier.

Using the savings strategy, the homeowner accumulates about $12,000 per year and eventually purchases a rental property. Their first property, a $350,000 rental, generates about $300 per month in cash flow after expenses. Instead of spending that income, they reinvest it along with ongoing savings, which allows them to purchase a second rental property a few years later. Over time, both properties appreciate and grow in value, eventually producing combined monthly cash flow of around $1,200 and steadily increasing.

By year 15, the difference between the two strategies becomes clear. Strategy A results in a fully paid-off home worth about $990,000 with no additional income streams. Strategy B results in approximately $1.6 million in total real estate equity, plus growing rental income and multiple assets working together. While the primary mortgage may not be fully paid off yet, the overall financial position is significantly larger and more diversified.

The key lesson is that both strategies work—but they produce different outcomes. Paying off the mortgage aggressively creates simplicity and emotional security, while balancing debt reduction with investing can potentially create greater long-term wealth, cash flow, and flexibility. The best approach depends on personal goals, risk tolerance, and whether the priority is maximum security or long-term income expansion.

Chapter 6

The Power of Compounding Real Estate Wealth — How Time Multiplies Equity, Cash Flow, and Financial Freedom

One of the most powerful forces in wealth creation is compounding. Compounding occurs when growth begins generating additional growth over time. Many people understand compounding in the context of savings accounts, retirement plans, or stock investments, but compounding inside real estate can become even more powerful because several wealth-building forces may operate simultaneously. Appreciation, mortgage amortization, rental income growth, tax advantages, inflation, and reinvestment can all work together over long periods to create substantial financial transformation.

Unfortunately, many people underestimate how dramatically time affects wealth. Modern culture often focuses on quick results, fast profits, and instant success. Social media frequently promotes stories of overnight millionaires, rapid house flipping, and aggressive investing strategies that appear glamorous. However, most lasting real estate wealth is built slowly through patience, discipline, and consistent decision-making over many years. Understanding the power of long-term compounding can completely change how homeowners and investors approach mortgage payoff and portfolio growth.

One of the biggest financial mistakes people make is focusing only on short-term results rather than long-term accumulation. For example, a homeowner may become discouraged because a rental property produces only a few hundred dollars per month in cash flow during the early years. However, they fail to realize that over time the mortgage balance declines, rents increase, appreciation compounds, and equity growth accelerates dramatically. Real estate wealth often appears slow at first and then accelerates significantly later because multiple compounding forces begin stacking on top of each other.

The first major compounding force in real estate is appreciation. Appreciation refers to the increase in property value over time. Although markets fluctuate in the short term, real estate values have historically trended upward over long periods due to inflation, population growth, wage increases, construction costs, and housing demand. A property appreciating at just 4 percent annually may not seem dramatic initially, but over decades the growth can become enormous because appreciation compounds on increasingly larger values. For example, a $300,000 property appreciating at 4 percent annually does not simply increase by $12,000 every year forever. In the second year, appreciation occurs on the new higher value. Over time, the annual dollar increase becomes larger and larger. This is the power of compounding appreciation. Investors who hold properties for long periods often benefit substantially from this effect.

The second major compounding force is mortgage amortization. Every monthly mortgage payment gradually reduces the loan balance. In the early years of a mortgage, a larger portion of the payment goes toward interest. Over time, more of each payment begins reducing principal. This means equity growth accelerates gradually even if property values remain stable. When tenants make rental payments, they effectively help reduce the investor's mortgage balance over time. This creates another layer of compounding wealth.

Many homeowners underestimate the significance of loan amortization because the progress initially feels slow. However, over ten, fifteen, or twenty years, the cumulative principal reduction can become substantial. When combined with appreciation, mortgage paydown creates a powerful long-term equity-building system.

The third compounding force is rental income growth. Inflation and housing demand often cause rents to increase gradually over time. Meanwhile, fixed-rate mortgage payments remain relatively stable. As rents rise while debt payments stay fixed, cash flow margins may expand significantly. This growing cash flow may then be reinvested into additional properties, mortgage reduction, reserves, retirement accounts, or other investments.

This is one reason many experienced investors focus heavily on long-term holds rather than short-term speculation. Properties that may produce moderate cash flow initially often become extremely profitable after years of rent growth combined with fixed financing costs. Patience allows the compounding process to work fully.

Inflation itself becomes another important compounding factor. Inflation gradually reduces the purchasing power of money over time. While inflation may increase costs in many areas of life, it may also benefit real estate owners in several ways. Property values and rents often rise during inflationary periods while long-term fixed-rate mortgage payments remain unchanged. In effect, inflation may reduce the real burden of mortgage debt over time because future dollars become less valuable.

This creates an interesting long-term dynamic. A mortgage payment that feels expensive today may become far easier to manage fifteen or twenty years later due to income growth and inflation. Investors who understand inflation often recognize the long-term value of controlling appreciating assets financed with fixed-rate debt.

Tax advantages may also compound wealth over time. Depreciation, mortgage interest deductions, expense write-offs, and potential capital gains strategies may improve after-tax returns significantly depending on individual circumstances and current tax laws. Reinvesting tax savings into additional investments or debt reduction may further accelerate long-term wealth growth.

Another important aspect of compounding is reinvestment. Small amounts of cash flow reinvested consistently over long periods may produce enormous results. For example, a rental property generating $400 per month in positive cash flow may not appear life-changing initially. However, if that cash flow is consistently reinvested into additional investments, mortgage reduction, or new acquisitions, the long-term impact becomes far greater than the original monthly amount alone.

This is why disciplined investors often avoid excessive lifestyle inflation during the early years of investing. Instead of immediately spending increasing cash flow on luxury purchases, they reinvest profits strategically to strengthen their financial systems. Over time, reinvested cash flow creates accelerating growth because each new asset or reduced debt balance contributes additional future financial benefits.

One of the greatest advantages of starting early is allowing compounding more time to operate. Time often matters more than speed. A modest portfolio built consistently over thirty years may dramatically outperform aggressive short-term speculation followed by financial instability. Investors who begin earlier usually benefit from longer periods of appreciation, amortization, rental growth, and reinvestment.

However, many people delay investing because they feel financially unprepared or fear making mistakes. While caution is important, excessive delay may carry significant opportunity cost. Waiting ten or fifteen years before purchasing investment properties may mean missing years of appreciation, mortgage paydown, and rental growth. Even one carefully selected property acquired earlier in life may produce substantial long-term wealth through compounding.

At the same time, compounding also applies negatively when financial mistakes repeat consistently. High-interest consumer debt, excessive spending, poor financial habits, and repeated refinancing for lifestyle consumption may compound financial stress over time. Just as positive decisions build momentum, negative decisions may gradually weaken long-term financial stability. This is why financial discipline becomes so important.

One of the most powerful emotional benefits of compounding real estate wealth is the gradual reduction of financial pressure. In the early years, many investors still rely heavily on employment income. However, as rental cash flow grows and debt balances decline, dependence on active income often decreases. Over time, investment income may begin covering larger portions of living expenses. Eventually, some investors reach the point where passive income covers most or all of their lifestyle needs.

This transition rarely happens suddenly. Instead, it often occurs gradually through years of consistent investing, debt management, and reinvestment. Many financially successful individuals eventually realize that wealth is not created through one dramatic event. It is usually built through small disciplined actions repeated over long periods.

Patience becomes essential because real estate cycles include both strong periods and difficult periods. Markets may slow temporarily. Property values may fluctuate. Expenses may rise unexpectedly. However, long-term investors who maintain strong cash flow and reserves are often better positioned to survive downturns and benefit from future recoveries. Compounding rewards those who can remain invested consistently over time.

Another important concept is scaling. As equity grows and cash flow improves, investors may gain access to additional financing opportunities or stronger purchasing power. Existing properties may help support future acquisitions through accumulated equity and cash flow. This creates a compounding portfolio effect where earlier investments help fund future growth.

However, scaling should always remain disciplined. Rapid uncontrolled growth fueled by excessive leverage often creates instability rather than freedom. Strong investors usually scale gradually while maintaining reserves, stable cash flow, and manageable debt obligations. The objective is sustainable growth capable of surviving long-term market cycles.

One reason many people underestimate compounding is because the early years often appear unimpressive. A rental property may initially produce modest cash flow while requiring maintenance, management, and patience. But after ten or twenty years, the combined effects of appreciation, loan amortization, rent growth, tax advantages, and reinvestment may become extraordinary. This delayed acceleration is one of the defining characteristics of compounding. The compounding effect becomes even more powerful when combined with mortgage payoff strategies. For example, rental cash flow may be used to accelerate primary mortgage reduction while the rental properties themselves continue appreciating and building equity. Eventually, homeowners may own multiple appreciating assets while simultaneously eliminating personal housing debt. This creates layered financial growth occurring in multiple directions at once.

Generational wealth is often built through compounding across decades rather than years. Properties held long term may eventually become fully paid off while continuing to generate rental income indefinitely. Appreciating assets may be passed to future generations, refinanced strategically, or used to support retirement income. Time transforms ordinary properties into potentially life-changing assets when managed wisely.

The most important lesson about compounding is understanding that consistency matters more than perfection. Investors do not need perfect market timing or extraordinary luck to benefit from compounding. They need patience, discipline, reasonable property selection, strong cash flow management, and long-term thinking. Small strategic decisions repeated consistently often create extraordinary financial outcomes over time. As you continue through this book, remember that every extra mortgage payment, every reserve contribution, every rental income deposit, and every investment decision becomes part of a larger compounding system. The earlier you begin building that system and the longer you maintain it responsibly, the more powerful the results may become.

Wealth is rarely built instantly. It is usually built quietly while time, appreciation, amortization, inflation, and reinvestment work together behind the scenes. The people who understand and respect the power of compounding often position themselves to achieve long-term financial freedom not through dramatic shortcuts but through disciplined consistency over many years.

How One Rental Property Can Compound Into Major Long-Term Wealth

Let's examine a realistic example of how appreciation, mortgage amortization, rental growth, and reinvestment may compound over time.

They didn't evaluate this property as a "$300 per month cash flow deal." They looked at it as a long-term wealth engine that would either quietly grow or quietly stagnate depending on how long they held it and how disciplined they remained. The property was purchased for $350,000 with a 20% down payment, leaving a $280,000 mortgage at 6.5% interest and a monthly payment of about $1,770.

At the start, the numbers look modest. The property rents for $3,000 per month, and after all expenses—including taxes, insurance, maintenance, vacancy reserves, and management fees—the investor is left with about $300 in positive cash flow. While small, this positive margin is important because it means the property is self-sustaining from day one instead of draining personal income.

Over time, two powerful forces begin to work together: appreciation and loan paydown. Assuming a 4% annual appreciation rate, the property grows from $350,000 to about $518,000 after 10 years, then to about $767,000 after 20 years, and potentially over $1.1 million after 30 years. At the same time, the mortgage balance steadily declines because tenants are effectively helping pay it down over time, eventually reaching zero.

By year 10, the property has already built approximately $282,000 in equity. By year 20, that grows to about $605,000, and by year 30, the investor owns a fully paid-off property worth over $1.1 million. This shows how time and tenant payments quietly transfer wealth from rent payments into equity ownership without requiring large additional effort from the investor. Meanwhile, rental income does not stay static. Assuming only a modest 3% annual rent increase, monthly rent grows from $3,000 to about $4,032 after 10 years, $5,418 after 20 years, and over $7,200 after 30 years. Even though expenses and the mortgage remain relatively stable, this rent growth gradually increases monthly cash flow from $300 to over $1,800 after 20 years and potentially $5,000+ per month once the mortgage is fully paid off.

In addition, the investor chooses to reinvest the initial $300 monthly cash flow into a simple investment account earning about 7% annually. Over 30 years, even this small starting amount grows to roughly $340,000. When combined with real estate equity of over $1.1 million and strong monthly cash flow, this single property has the potential to generate over $1.4 million in total wealth impact.

The key lesson is that real estate wealth is not created in the first year—it is created through time. Early returns may look small, but appreciation, rent growth, loan amortization, and reinvestment compound quietly in the background. The real power of a rental property is not just in monthly cash flow, but in its ability to transform consistent, long-term ownership into significant equity, income, and financial freedom over decades.

Chapter 7

Building Financial Freedom Through Multiple Streams of Real Estate Income

One of the greatest advantages of real estate investing is the ability to create multiple streams of income from assets that may continue producing cash flow for decades. Most people begin their financial journey relying almost entirely on one source of income, usually a job or business. While employment income can provide stability, relying on a single source of income may create financial vulnerability. If the job disappears, hours are reduced, health problems arise, or economic conditions change, financial stress can appear quickly. Building multiple streams of real estate income helps reduce dependence on a single paycheck while increasing long-term flexibility, security, and opportunity.

Financial freedom is often misunderstood. Many people believe financial freedom simply means becoming rich or owning expensive things. In reality, financial freedom is usually about control and flexibility. It means having enough income-producing assets to support your lifestyle without depending entirely on active work. It means having options. It means reducing financial stress and increasing your ability to make decisions based on values, goals, and priorities rather than fear or immediate financial pressure.

Real estate can become one of the most effective tools for building multiple streams of income because a single property may generate wealth in several ways simultaneously. Rental income, appreciation, mortgage amortization, tax benefits, inflation protection, refinancing opportunities, and business-related income may all develop from real estate ownership over time. When these income streams are organized strategically, they may create a financial system capable of supporting long-term independence and wealth.

The first and most obvious stream of real estate income is monthly rental cash flow. Rental income is the foundation of many successful real estate portfolios because it provides recurring monthly revenue. When a property is purchased correctly, rental income may exceed the total monthly expenses associated with the property, including mortgage payments, taxes, insurance, maintenance, management, and reserves. The remaining amount becomes positive cash flow.

Even modest cash flow may become extremely powerful when multiplied across several properties and allowed to grow over time. For example, a property producing only $300 per month in positive cash flow may not seem impressive initially. However, five properties generating $300 each produce

$1,500 per month. Over time, as rents rise and mortgage balances decline, the cash flow may increase substantially. Eventually, the combined rental income may cover large portions of personal living expenses or replace employment income entirely.

Another important stream of real estate income comes from loan amortization. Every mortgage payment gradually reduces the principal balance on the property loan. In effect, tenants help build the investor's equity through their rental payments. Although this equity growth may not immediately appear as spendable cash, it increases net worth steadily over time. Many investors underestimate how powerful mortgage paydown becomes after ten, fifteen, or twenty years of ownership.

Appreciation creates another major wealth-building stream. Property values often increase over long periods due to inflation, population growth, limited housing supply, rising construction costs, and economic expansion. Appreciation may dramatically increase net worth over time, especially when combined with leverage. Because real estate investors control large assets using financing, appreciation occurs on the full property value rather than only the cash invested. This creates the potential for accelerated long-term wealth growth. Tax benefits may also function as an indirect income stream.

Real estate investors often receive deductions related to mortgage interest, depreciation, repairs, insurance, management fees, travel expenses, property taxes, and other operational costs. These deductions may reduce taxable income and improve after-tax cash flow. Depending on the investor's situation, tax savings may be reinvested into additional investments, debt reduction, reserves, or retirement planning.

Inflation protection is another frequently overlooked financial advantage. As inflation increases over time, rents and property values often rise as well. Fixed-rate mortgage payments, however, remain relatively stable. This means that inflation may gradually improve cash flow margins while reducing the real burden of long-term mortgage debt. Investors who own appreciating assets financed with fixed-rate loans may benefit significantly during inflationary periods.

One of the most powerful concepts in real estate wealth building is stacking income streams. Instead of relying on a single financial benefit, real estate allows several forms of wealth creation to operate simultaneously. A rental property may generate monthly cash flow while also appreciating in value, reducing its mortgage balance, providing tax advantages, and increasing future refinancing flexibility. These layered benefits often create much stronger long-term results than relying on only one financial strategy alone. Refinancing opportunities may create additional financial flexibility as equity grows. Investors sometimes refinance properties strategically to lower interest rates, improve cash flow, consolidate debt, or access equity for additional investments. When managed carefully, refinancing may allow investors to expand portfolios without selling appreciating assets. However, refinancing should always be approached conservatively and supported by strong cash flow and reserves.

Some investors create additional streams of real estate-related income through active services connected to the industry. Property management, short-term rental hosting, real estate consulting, renovation services, mortgage brokerage, bookkeeping, photography, staging, construction, and real estate education may all generate supplemental income connected to property ownership experience. These additional business streams may strengthen overall financial stability while expanding professional opportunities.

Short-term rentals may also provide higher income potential in certain markets. Properties used for vacation rentals or furnished short-term housing may generate significantly higher gross rental income than traditional long-term leases. However, short-term rentals often involve greater management intensity, higher turnover, more variable occupancy, local regulations, and operational complexity. Investors should evaluate whether the increased income potential justifies the additional work and risk.

House hacking remains one of the most accessible ways to begin building multiple real estate income streams. House hacking involves using a primary residence to generate rental income by renting rooms, basement apartments, guest houses, duplex units, or multifamily spaces. This strategy may significantly reduce or eliminate personal housing expenses while allowing homeowners to build investment experience gradually. Many financially successful investors began their journey through simple house hacking strategies before acquiring larger portfolios.

Another important concept is income diversification. Relying heavily on a single tenant, property type, or market may increase financial vulnerability. Diversification may involve owning different property types, operating in multiple neighborhoods, maintaining multiple tenants, or combining long-term and short-term rental strategies. Diversified income streams often provide greater stability during economic shifts because weakness in one area may be offset by strength in another.

However, diversification should not become overcomplication. Many inexperienced investors pursue too many strategies simultaneously without mastering any of them properly. Sustainable investing often involves building gradually and maintaining operational simplicity whenever possible. Strong systems, manageable properties, reliable tenants, and consistent cash flow are usually more valuable than complicated portfolios producing excessive stress.

One of the greatest emotional benefits of multiple income streams is reduced financial anxiety. When people rely entirely on employment income, unexpected disruptions may feel catastrophic. But when rental properties and other investments begin generating consistent cash flow, financial pressure often decreases gradually. Investors gain confidence knowing their financial system no longer depends entirely on one paycheck.

Over time, multiple streams of income may create significant lifestyle flexibility. Some investors reduce work hours, transition careers, start businesses, spend more time with family, travel more frequently, or retire earlier because passive income provides additional support. Financial freedom often emerges gradually as income-producing assets slowly replace dependence on active labor.

At the same time, building multiple streams of income requires patience and discipline. Most real estate investors do not achieve financial independence quickly. Properties require management, repairs, reserves, financing analysis, and long-term planning. Cash flow may appear modest during the early years. Appreciation may fluctuate. Tenants may create occasional challenges. The key is maintaining realistic expectations while focusing on consistent long-term growth.

One common mistake people make is increasing personal spending too quickly as rental income grows. Lifestyle inflation can significantly slow wealth creation. Instead of reinvesting growing cash flow into additional assets, reserves, mortgage reduction, or retirement accounts, some investors immediately increase personal expenses. While enjoying financial progress is important, excessive lifestyle inflation may weaken long-term compounding benefits.

Strong reserves remain critically important even after building multiple income streams. Properties will eventually require repairs, turnovers, maintenance, and unexpected expenses. Economic cycles may temporarily reduce occupancy or rental demand. Investors who maintain healthy reserves are usually better positioned to navigate uncertainty calmly and continue benefiting from long-term property ownership.

Another important lesson is understanding the difference between gross income and true cash flow. A property generating high rent may still perform poorly if expenses are excessive. Sustainable wealth comes from net cash flow after realistic operating costs, reserves, taxes, and financing expenses are included. Conservative analysis protects investors from unpleasant surprises and improves long-term stability.

Time remains one of the most powerful components of financial freedom. The earlier income-producing assets are acquired and managed responsibly, the more time appreciation, loan amortization, inflation, and rental growth have to compound. Many investors become financially successful not because they earned extraordinary incomes but because they consistently acquired and held appreciating assets over long periods.

Real estate wealth also becomes increasingly powerful when debt obligations begin declining. Properties that once produced modest cash flow may become highly profitable after mortgages are paid down significantly or eliminated entirely. A portfolio of fully or partially paid-off rental properties may create substantial retirement income while continuing to appreciate over time.

Generational wealth often develops through these long-term income systems. Properties acquired decades earlier may eventually provide income for children, grandchildren, or future family opportunities. Real estate may support education, business investments, retirement security, or inheritance planning across generations when managed wisely. Ultimately, building multiple streams of real estate income is not simply about money. It is about creating options, reducing stress, increasing stability, and gaining greater control over your future. Financial freedom rarely appears suddenly. It is usually built slowly through consistent investment, disciplined management, long-term ownership, and patient reinvestment.

As you continue through this book, remember that every property, every mortgage payment, every reserve contribution, and every rental check may become part of a larger financial ecosystem. Over time, multiple streams of income working together may gradually transform your financial life in ways that initially seemed impossible.

The process requires patience, education, and discipline, but the long-term rewards may include far more than financial gain alone. Real estate income streams may eventually provide freedom of time, freedom of choice, and the ability to build a more secure future for yourself and the people you care about most.

Building Multiple Streams of Real Estate Income Over 20 Years

They didn't start this journey trying to "build a real estate portfolio." They started with a much simpler goal: buy a home, add one rental property, and create more financial stability than relying on a paycheck alone. The starting point was two properties—a primary residence worth $500,000 with a $400,000 mortgage, and a rental property purchased for $300,000 with a $240,000 loan at 6.5% interest.

At first glance, the numbers look fairly normal. The primary home costs about $2,271 per month, while the rental property brings in $2,700 in rent and produces about $373 in monthly positive cash flow after all expenses. Nothing about the first year looks life-changing. In fact, most of the early benefit is simply that the property is self-sustaining rather than draining money.

Over time, however, multiple financial forces begin working together. Rent gradually increases at about 3% per year, while the mortgage payment remains mostly fixed. After 20 years, rent grows to nearly $4,900 per month, while expenses only increase slightly. This turns a small $373 monthly profit into roughly $1,677 per month in positive cash flow from just one property.

At the same time, tenants are slowly paying down the mortgage, reducing the loan balance from $240,000 to about $139,000 over 20 years. Meanwhile, the property appreciates at about 4% annually, growing from $300,000 to roughly $657,000. When you combine appreciation with debt reduction, the investor builds about $518,000 in equity from this single rental property alone.

On top of that, the investor benefits from tax advantages such as depreciation, interest deductions, and expense write-offs, which generate around $3,000 per year in tax savings. Over 20 years, that adds up to more than $60,000, which if reinvested grows to roughly $123,000. In addition, the original rental cash flow is also reinvested over time, growing into another $183,000.

When everything is combined, one rental property creates multiple layers of wealth simultaneously: equity growth, cash flow, tax benefits, and reinvestment growth. After 20 years, the total measurable financial impact exceeds $824,000, not including future appreciation or continued income growth. The key lesson is that real estate wealth is rarely built from a single factor—it is created when time, leverage, rent growth, tax advantages, and disciplined reinvestment all compound together consistently over many years.

Chapter 8

Risk Management and Financial Protection — How to Build Wealth Without Losing It

One of the most overlooked aspects of wealth creation is risk management. Many people spend enormous amounts of time learning how to make money, invest money, or grow assets, yet very few spend enough time learning how to protect the wealth they build. In real estate investing, protecting wealth is just as important as creating it. A portfolio that grows rapidly without proper safeguards may become financially unstable during market downturns, economic recessions, vacancies, lawsuits, rising interest rates, or unexpected personal emergencies. Sustainable financial freedom is built not only through growth but also through protection, discipline, and preparation.

One of the biggest differences between long-term successful investors and struggling investors is how they manage risk. Successful investors do not assume everything will always go perfectly. Instead, they plan for uncertainty before problems appear. They understand that real estate markets move in cycles, tenants may create challenges, repairs are inevitable, interest rates fluctuate, and life circumstances may change unexpectedly. Rather than ignoring these realities, disciplined investors build financial systems capable of absorbing setbacks without collapsing.

Many inexperienced investors become overly focused on excitement, appreciation projections, or aggressive growth strategies while neglecting the fundamentals of financial protection. During strong markets, rapid appreciation may create the illusion that risk no longer matters. Investors may borrow heavily, reduce reserves, overestimate future rents, or purchase properties with weak cash flow assumptions because they believe property values will continue rising forever. However, markets eventually shift, and when they do, investors without strong risk management systems often experience significant financial stress.

Risk management begins with understanding that real estate investing is a business. Every business carries risk. Rental properties require management, maintenance, financing, insurance, legal compliance, and long-term planning. Investors who approach real estate casually often make emotional decisions that weaken long-term stability. Investors who treat their properties like businesses usually make more disciplined and sustainable decisions. One of the most important principles of risk management is maintaining adequate reserves. Reserves are accessible cash funds set aside specifically for emergencies, repairs, vacancies, unexpected expenses, or temporary income disruptions. Reserves provide flexibility and reduce the likelihood of panic-driven decisions during difficult situations.

Many investors underestimate how frequently unexpected expenses occur in real estate. Roofs eventually wear out. Air conditioning systems fail. Plumbing leaks happen. Appliances break. Tenants move out unexpectedly. Insurance premiums rise. Property taxes increase. Economic downturns may reduce rental demand temporarily. Investors without reserves often rely on credit cards, high-interest loans, or emotional decisions when problems arise. Strong reserves help prevent temporary setbacks from becoming financial disasters.

A common recommendation among experienced investors is maintaining at least six to twelve months of total expenses for each property owned. This may include mortgage payments, taxes, insurance, utilities if applicable, and estimated maintenance costs. Some investors maintain even larger reserves during uncertain economic conditions or when managing higher-risk properties.

Liquidity is closely connected to reserves. Liquidity refers to how quickly assets can be converted into accessible cash. A person may appear wealthy on paper because of large amounts of home equity or property appreciation, yet still struggle financially if they lack liquid funds. Real estate is generally not a highly liquid asset because properties may take time to refinance or sell. Maintaining liquid reserves allows investors to respond quickly to opportunities and emergencies without depending entirely on borrowing or forced property sales.

Another major area of risk management involves cash flow analysis. Cash flow protects investors during difficult periods because properties producing positive cash flow may continue supporting themselves even when markets soften. Investors who purchase properties based entirely on appreciation expectations often face greater risk because appreciation is not guaranteed in the short term. Cash flow creates stability and holding power.

Conservative cash flow analysis is especially important. Many inexperienced investors underestimate expenses or overestimate rental income when evaluating deals. Successful investors typically use conservative assumptions for vacancies, maintenance, repairs, rent growth, and future costs. Conservative analysis may occasionally cause investors to reject borderline deals, but it also reduces the likelihood of unpleasant surprises later.

Interest rate risk must also be managed carefully. Adjustable-rate financing, HELOCs, and short-term loans may become significantly more expensive when interest rates rise. Investors relying heavily on variable-rate debt may experience sudden increases in monthly payments that weaken cash flow dramatically. Fixed-rate financing often provides greater long-term stability because payments remain predictable regardless of future interest rate changes.

Leverage itself represents both opportunity and risk. Real estate allows investors to control large assets using borrowed money, which may accelerate wealth creation significantly during strong periods. However, excessive leverage may create financial vulnerability. Investors with very high debt obligations relative to cash flow or reserves may struggle during vacancies, market corrections, or income disruptions.

One of the safest long-term investing strategies involves moderate leverage combined with strong cash flow and reserves. Sustainable investors focus less on maximizing short-term growth and more on creating portfolios capable of surviving long-term market cycles. Wealth is often built gradually through consistent ownership rather than rapid speculative expansion.

Diversification may also reduce risk. Relying heavily on one property, one tenant, one market, or one income source may create vulnerability. Diversification can involve owning multiple properties, investing in different neighborhoods, maintaining different property types, or building additional income streams outside of real estate. Diversified income sources may provide greater stability during changing market conditions.

However, diversification should remain strategic rather than chaotic. Some investors overcomplicate their portfolios by pursuing too many investment strategies simultaneously. Simplicity often improves risk management because it allows investors to focus more effectively on operations, cash flow, and financial oversight.

Insurance becomes another critical layer of protection. Property insurance, liability insurance, umbrella coverage, flood insurance when appropriate, and landlord policies may all help protect against financial loss. Many investors underestimate liability risk until legal problems occur. Lawsuits, tenant injuries, property damage, and natural disasters may create enormous financial exposure without adequate coverage.

Legal structure also matters. Depending on the investor's situation, properties may be held personally or through legal entities such as LLCs. Legal structures may provide liability protection, operational flexibility, and organizational benefits when implemented properly. Investors should work with qualified legal and tax professionals when evaluating entity structures and asset protection planning.

Tenant screening is another major aspect of risk management. Poor tenant selection may lead to missed payments, property damage, legal disputes, evictions, and financial stress. Successful landlords usually develop clear tenant qualification standards involving credit history, income verification, rental history, background checks, and communication evaluation. Careful tenant screening often prevents many future problems.

Maintenance should also be approached proactively rather than reactively. Deferred maintenance often becomes more expensive over time. Regular inspections, preventive repairs, and property upkeep may reduce larger future costs while preserving property value and tenant satisfaction. Well-maintained properties often attract stronger tenants and experience lower turnover rates.

Another important concept is avoiding emotional investing. Fear and greed frequently cause poor financial decisions.

During rapidly rising markets, greed may tempt investors into overpaying for properties, using excessive leverage, or ignoring weak cash flow. During downturns, fear may cause investors to sell properties prematurely or avoid opportunities entirely. Strong risk management systems help reduce emotional decision-making by creating clear financial guidelines and discipline.

Economic cycles are unavoidable. Real estate markets move through periods of expansion, contraction, recovery, and stabilization. Investors who understand cycles often prepare for downturns during strong periods rather than assuming current conditions will continue forever. This preparation may involve increasing reserves, reducing leverage gradually, improving cash flow, or avoiding overly aggressive acquisitions during overheated markets.

Job loss and personal income disruptions also represent important risks. Many real estate investors initially depend heavily on employment income to support mortgages and investments. Losing employment income unexpectedly may create pressure if reserves and cash flow are insufficient. Building multiple streams of income and maintaining manageable obligations may reduce this vulnerability over time.

Health emergencies and family changes should also be considered. Disability, illness, divorce, caregiving responsibilities, or unexpected life transitions may significantly affect finances. Investors who build flexible financial systems often navigate personal challenges more successfully because they maintain reserves, insurance, and lower financial stress.

One of the greatest advantages of strong risk management is emotional stability. Investors with healthy reserves, strong cash flow, conservative financing, and manageable debt often experience less financial anxiety because they know their systems can absorb setbacks. This emotional confidence allows them to make clearer long-term decisions rather than reacting impulsively during stressful situations.

Risk management does not eliminate uncertainty completely. Every investment carries some level of uncertainty. However, proper preparation dramatically improves the ability to survive challenges and continue building wealth over time. Financial success is not usually determined by avoiding all problems. It is often determined by how well investors respond when problems inevitably occur.

Another important lesson is understanding that protecting wealth becomes increasingly important as wealth grows.

During the early stages of investing, people often focus primarily on growth and acquisition. Over time, preserving cash flow, protecting equity, minimizing unnecessary risk, and maintaining stability become equally important. Long-term financial freedom depends on both growth and protection working together.

Some of the most financially successful investors in history were not necessarily the most aggressive. Many succeeded because they remained disciplined, avoided catastrophic mistakes, survived downturns, and continued compounding wealth steadily over decades. Avoiding financial destruction is often more important than chasing maximum short-term returns.

Ultimately, risk management allows investors to stay in the game long enough for compounding to work fully. Appreciation, mortgage amortization, rental growth, and reinvestment require time. Investors forced to sell properties prematurely due to poor planning often lose the opportunity to benefit from long-term compounding.

As you continue through this book, remember that financial freedom is not built only through acquisition and growth. It is built through stability, preparation, and intelligent protection. Strong reserves, conservative cash flow analysis, disciplined leverage, diversification, insurance, and long-term planning may not appear exciting, but they often form the true foundation of lasting wealth.

The goal is not to eliminate all risk completely. The goal is to manage risk intelligently so that temporary setbacks do not permanently destroy long-term opportunity. Investors who respect risk rather than ignore it are often the ones who ultimately achieve sustainable financial freedom.

How Strong Risk Management Can Protect a Real Estate Portfolio During a Downturn

Let's walk through a realistic example that shows how two investors can follow completely different strategies and end up with very different outcomes when unexpected challenges hit the market.

Both Investor A and Investor B purchase identical rental properties for $400,000 that rent for $3,500 per month. On the surface, both deals look solid and cash-flow positive. However, the difference between them is not the property—it is how they structure risk, leverage, and reserves from the very beginning.

Investor A chooses an aggressive approach. They put only 10% down ($40,000) and finance the rest with a $360,000 loan at 7% interest. Their monthly mortgage payment is about $2,395.

After taxes, insurance, management fees, and minimal reserves, the property produces about $315 in monthly cash flow. However, they only keep about $2,000 in total emergency savings, leaving them highly exposed if anything goes wrong.

Investor B takes a more conservative approach. They put 25% down ($100,000), reducing their loan to $300,000 at 6.5% interest. Their monthly mortgage payment is lower at about $1,896. Even though they earn slightly less leverage, they build stronger protection into the deal with higher maintenance and vacancy reserves. Their property produces about $514 in monthly cash flow, and they maintain $25,000 in emergency reserves.

After two years of stable performance, an unexpected economic downturn occurs. The tenant loses their job and stops paying rent. The property sits vacant for four months, and at the same time, an $8,000 air conditioning replacement is required. Insurance premiums also increase by 15%, adding further pressure to monthly expenses.

For Investor A, the situation becomes extremely difficult. During the four-month vacancy, they must still cover about $3,185 per month in expenses, totaling roughly $12,740. Adding the $8,000 repair brings total unexpected costs to about \$20,740. With only \$2,000 in reserves, they face a shortfall of nearly \$18,740. To survive, they may be forced to rely on credit cards, take on high-interest debt, miss payments, or even consider selling the property under financial stress.

Investor B experiences the same challenges but in a very different way. Their monthly expenses are lower at about \$2,986, totaling roughly \$11,944 over the same vacancy period. Adding the \$8,000 repair brings their total unexpected cost to about \$19,944. However, because they maintained \$25,000 in reserves, they are able to cover all expenses and still keep about \$5,000 in savings remaining.

Once the market stabilizes, both properties recover. New tenants move in, rents gradually increase again, and appreciation resumes. Investor B continues building wealth through steady cash flow, loan amortization, and long-term appreciation, without interruption. Investor A, however, may have lost years of progress due to financial strain, forced decisions, or damaged credit.

The key lesson is not that leverage is bad—it is that risk management determines survival. Investor A took more risk but lacked protection. Investor B accepted slightly lower short-term gains but built a system that could withstand real-world shocks. Over time, the investors who survive downturns are the ones who ultimately benefit most from long-term appreciation, compounding, and financial freedom.

Chapter 9

The Strategic Exit Plan – Knowing When to Pay Down Debt and When to Scale Your Portfolio

One of the most advanced concepts in real estate wealth building is understanding when to prioritize mortgage payoff and when to prioritize portfolio expansion. Many investors operate without a clear exit strategy, which leads to inconsistent decisions, emotional investing, and inefficient use of capital over time. Some people aggressively pay down their primary mortgage while missing investment opportunities that could have generated long-term cash flow. Others scale too quickly into multiple properties without ever stabilizing their financial foundation or reducing personal liabilities. The strategic exit plan is the ability to intentionally shift between debt reduction and asset accumulation based on financial position, market conditions, and long-term goals. This is where true wealth strategy begins to separate from basic financial behavior.

A strategic exit plan is not about timing the market perfectly. It is about understanding financial phases. In the early phase of wealth building, cash flow and asset acquisition may matter more than aggressive mortgage payoff. In the middle phase, investors often begin balancing debt reduction with portfolio stabilization. In the later phase, mortgage payoff, cash flow optimization, and risk reduction become more important than aggressive expansion. These phases are not fixed by age but by financial position, income stability, equity levels, and risk tolerance. Investors who understand this cycle make more effective long-term decisions.

One of the most important mistakes people make is applying a single financial strategy forever. For example, someone may decide early in life that all extra income should go toward paying off their mortgage. While this may feel safe, it can significantly limit long-term wealth potential if applied too rigidly for decades. On the other hand, an investor who only focuses on acquiring properties without ever reducing debt may create unnecessary financial stress and vulnerability. A strategic exit plan allows for flexibility between both approaches.

The key driver of the exit plan is cash flow strength. When personal income is strong and stable, investors may feel more comfortable allocating funds toward investment properties. When cash flow becomes tighter or when market conditions become uncertain, shifting focus toward debt reduction and liquidity may become more appropriate. This dynamic approach ensures that financial decisions remain aligned with real-world conditions rather than fixed rules.

Another major factor is equity positioning. As equity grows in both primary residences and investment properties, financial flexibility increases. However, equity alone does not create cash flow. Investors must decide how to deploy equity strategically. In some cases, equity may be used to acquire additional properties. In others, it may be used to reduce debt and improve financial stability. The strategic exit plan evaluates equity not as a static number but as a flexible resource that can support multiple financial objectives.

Market cycles also play a critical role in exit planning. During strong appreciation cycles, investors may prioritize expansion and acquisition. During slower or uncertain markets, they may prioritize debt reduction and cash flow stabilization. Understanding where the market is in its cycle helps investors avoid emotional decisions such as overpaying for properties during peak conditions or panic-selling during downturns. A disciplined investor aligns strategy with cycles rather than reacting emotionally to short-term changes.

Tax strategy becomes increasingly important in advanced exit planning. Real estate investors may benefit from depreciation, interest deductions, expense write-offs, and long-term capital gains treatment. However, tax efficiency should never be the sole reason for making investment decisions. Instead, tax benefits should be viewed as enhancements to already sound investment strategies. A strong exit plan considers after-tax returns, not just gross income or appreciation.

Another important aspect of the exit strategy is lifestyle alignment. Financial success is not only about numbers. It is about the life those numbers support. Some investors want early retirement. Others want passive income while continuing to work. Some prioritize generational wealth. Others prioritize financial independence without excessive complexity. The exit plan must align with personal values to remain sustainable over time.

Liquidity remains a core pillar of strategic planning. Investors often underestimate how important cash reserves become as portfolios grow. Unexpected repairs, vacancies, legal issues, or economic downturns can create financial strain without sufficient liquidity. A strong exit plan always includes reserve planning as a permanent requirement, not an optional step. Liquidity provides stability and ensures that investors can hold assets long enough to benefit from long-term compounding.

One of the most powerful concepts in this chapter is controlled scaling. Controlled scaling means growing a portfolio at a pace that does not compromise financial stability. Instead of aggressively acquiring properties as fast as possible, controlled scaling focuses on sustainable growth supported by cash flow, reserves, and disciplined leverage. This approach ensures that each new asset strengthens the financial system rather than destabilizing it.

Debt optimization is also a key component of the exit strategy. Not all debt should be eliminated immediately, and not all debt should be maintained indefinitely. Strategic investors analyze interest rates, amortization schedules, cash flow impact, and opportunity cost before deciding how to manage each loan. Sometimes paying down debt aggressively is optimal. Other times, maintaining low-interest debt while investing excess capital may create superior long-term outcomes.

The ultimate goal of the strategic exit plan is flexibility. Financial freedom is not a single destination but a range of options. A well-designed exit strategy allows investors to choose between reducing debt, expanding portfolios, increasing cash flow, or transitioning toward retirement depending on life circumstances. Without a plan, investors often default into reactive decision-making. With a plan, investors operate intentionally and confidently.

As investors progress through different financial stages, the exit plan evolves. Early stages focus on acquisition and leverage. Middle stages focus on balance and optimization. Later stages focus on stability, income, and preservation. The ability to shift between these stages smoothly is what separates long-term successful investors from inconsistent ones.

Ultimately, the strategic exit plan ensures that mortgage payoff and real estate investing are not competing goals but integrated parts of a single financial system. Instead of asking "Should I pay off my mortgage or invest?", the advanced investor asks "What combination of payoff, investment, and liquidity creates the strongest long-term outcome right now?" This mindset shift is what allows wealth to compound intelligently over time.

Real-Life Math Example — Strategic Exit Decision Over 10 Years

They didn't approach their finances as a debate between two opposing strategies. Instead, they zoomed in on a single opportunity: an extra $2,000 per month in consistent cash flow. With a $600,000 home, a $400,000 mortgage at 5.5%, and a stable payment of $2,271, they already had a strong position—the real question was how that additional money would shape their financial future over time.

In Scenario A, the homeowner chooses a pure debt-elimination strategy. They apply the full $2,000 per month toward the mortgage, which totals $240,000 in extra payments over 10 years. This approach aggressively reduces debt and puts them on track to eliminate the mortgage in about 13 years. However, no additional investments or income-producing assets are created during this time. After 10 years, they have strong home equity—around $500,000 to $550,000—but no secondary income streams or diversified wealth.

In Scenario B, the homeowner chooses a more balanced wealth strategy. Instead of focusing only on debt reduction, they split the $2,000 monthly surplus—$1,000 goes toward the mortgage and $1,000 goes into investments. Over 10 years, this still results in about $120,000 in extra mortgage payments, but it also allows capital to grow separately through investing. At a 7% return, the investment account grows to approximately $174,000, creating a second layer of wealth beyond the home.

After about three years of consistent saving, this second strategy also allows the homeowner to enter real estate investing. They use accumulated funds for an $80,000 down payment on a $350,000 rental property. This property generates initial cash flow of about $300 per month and builds equity over time. After 10 years, the rental property grows to approximately $520,000 in value, with about $270,000 in equity after accounting for the remaining mortgage.

When combining all assets after 10 years, the difference becomes clear. Scenario A produces a single outcome: roughly $500,000–$550,000 in home equity with no additional income streams. Scenario B produces a diversified portfolio: about $450,000 in home equity, $270,000 in rental equity, and $174,000 in investments, plus growing monthly cash flow from the rental property. Total combined wealth impact reaches approximately $894,000 or more.

The key lesson is that aggressive mortgage payoff builds strong security in a single asset, while a strategic exit plan builds multiple wealth engines at the same time. One approach focuses on eliminating debt, while the other focuses on building income, equity, and liquidity simultaneously. Over time, diversification often creates greater financial flexibility and long-term resilience, even if progress feels slower at the beginning.

Chapter 10

The Ultimate Wealth Integration System — Combining Mortgage Payoff, Investing, Cash Flow, and Freedom Planning

The final stage of financial mastery is not choosing between mortgage payoff or real estate investing, but integrating both into a unified wealth system. Most people treat these financial goals as separate paths, often believing they must choose one over the other. However, advanced investors understand that mortgage payoff, portfolio growth, cash flow generation, and liquidity management are not competing strategies. They are interconnected components of a single financial ecosystem designed to build long-term freedom.

The ultimate wealth integration system begins with clarity. Without clarity, financial decisions become reactive and inconsistent. Some months the focus is debt reduction, other months it is investing, and other times it is saving or spending without structure. Integration creates alignment. Every dollar is assigned a role within a broader system that supports long-term goals rather than short-term impulses. The foundation of this system is income allocation. Income must be divided strategically between four primary categories: mortgage reduction, investment growth, reserves, and lifestyle. When income is allocated intentionally, financial progress becomes predictable rather than random. This structure ensures that every financial priority receives attention consistently over time.

Mortgage payoff remains an important component of the system, but it is no longer the only focus. Instead, mortgage reduction becomes one of several parallel strategies. Some portion of income is directed toward reducing debt, while another portion is directed toward acquiring income-producing assets. This dual approach allows investors to improve both financial stability and long-term wealth simultaneously.

Cash flow is the central engine of the integration system. Without cash flow, financial systems rely heavily on external income such as salaries or business revenue. With cash flow, financial systems begin to operate independently. Rental income, business income, and investment returns begin supporting expenses, debt payments, and additional investments. Over time, cash flow reduces dependence on active work.

Reserves act as the stability layer. Without reserves, even strong income systems may fail under stress. Reserves protect against unexpected expenses, vacancies, economic downturns, and personal emergencies. A strong wealth system always includes liquidity as a permanent requirement rather than a temporary step.

Leverage becomes the acceleration mechanism. When used responsibly, leverage allows investors to control larger assets with less initial capital. However, leverage must always be balanced with cash flow and reserves. The goal is not to maximize debt but to optimize it. Proper leverage allows wealth to grow faster without creating instability.

One of the most important principles in the integration system is feedback loops. Positive cash flow increases reserves. Increased reserves allow for safer investments. Safer investments generate additional cash flow. Additional cash flow accelerates mortgage payoff. Mortgage reduction improves stability and borrowing capacity. Each component strengthens the others when managed correctly.

Time is the most powerful force in this system. Over short periods, results may appear modest. However, over long periods, compounding effects create exponential growth. Appreciation, amortization, rent increases, reinvestment, and debt reduction all multiply each other over time. The longer the system operates, the more powerful it becomes.

The integration system also emphasizes adaptability. Financial life is not static. Income changes, markets shift, interest rates fluctuate, and personal priorities evolve. A strong system allows adjustments without breaking structure. For example, during economic uncertainty, more income may be allocated toward reserves and mortgage stability. During strong markets, more may be allocated toward investment expansion.

Emotional control is another essential component. Financial decisions driven by fear or greed often lead to inconsistency. Fear may cause investors to avoid opportunities or overpay debt too aggressively. Greed may cause overleveraging or risky investments. The integration system replaces emotional decision-making with structured allocation rules that remain consistent regardless of market conditions.

Lifestyle planning is also part of integration. Wealth is not only about accumulation but also about quality of life. A successful system allows individuals to enjoy financial progress without undermining long-term goals. Controlled lifestyle spending ensures that financial freedom improves gradually without sacrificing future stability.

The ultimate goal of the wealth integration system is financial independence. Financial independence occurs when passive income, investments, and reserves are sufficient to support lifestyle needs without reliance on active employment income. This does not necessarily require eliminating all debt immediately or owning hundreds of properties. Instead, it requires building enough income-producing assets to create consistent financial coverage.

As the system matures, mortgage payoff often accelerates naturally through accumulated cash flow and investment income. Instead of forcing aggressive payoff from limited income, the system allows debt reduction to occur as a result of expanding financial capacity. This creates a more sustainable and less stressful approach to wealth building.

In later stages, many investors shift focus from accumulation to optimization. Instead of aggressively acquiring new assets, they focus on improving cash flow, reducing inefficiencies, eliminating unnecessary debt, and preserving wealth. This transition is a natural part of financial evolution.

Ultimately, the integration system transforms financial planning from isolated decisions into a connected structure. Every mortgage payment, investment decision, reserve contribution, and cash flow allocation becomes part of a larger system designed to build long-term freedom. This approach removes confusion and replaces it with clarity and purpose. The most successful investors are not those who choose one strategy over another, but those who learn how to combine multiple strategies into one cohesive system. Mortgage payoff, investing, cash flow, leverage, reserves, and lifestyle planning all work together rather than compete.

Financial freedom is not achieved by focusing on a single goal. It is achieved by building a system where all financial components work together over time to create stability, flexibility, and long-term wealth.

Real-Life Math Example – Full Wealth Integration Over 15 Years

They didn't begin by trying to "optimize everything at once." Instead, they started with a simple but powerful decision: how to intentionally divide $3,000 per month so every dollar had a clear purpose. With consistent income available for allocation, the goal was not just to reduce debt—but to build a system where multiple financial priorities could grow at the same time.

From the start, they committed to a structured allocation plan: $1,000 toward mortgage reduction, $1,000 toward long-term investing, $500 toward reserves, and $500 toward a flexible lifestyle buffer. This balanced approach ensured that progress wasn't happening in just one area, but across all key parts of their financial life simultaneously. On the mortgage side, the $1,000 monthly extra payment created a powerful acceleration effect. Over 15 years, this adds up to $180,000 in additional principal reduction, shortening the mortgage by roughly 12 to 15 years and significantly reducing total interest paid. Instead of simply "paying faster," they were reshaping the entire payoff timeline.

At the same time, the investment portion was working quietly in the background. By consistently investing $1,000 per month at an estimated 7% return, the portfolio grows to approximately $315,000 over 15 years. This creates a second major asset base that grows independently of the home.

The reserve strategy adds another layer of stability. By saving $500 per month, the homeowner builds a financial cushion of about $130,000 over time. This reserve account protects against emergencies, job changes, or unexpected expenses, ensuring that the entire system remains stable even during financial stress. In addition, after about four years, accumulated savings allow them to purchase a rental property, which grows over 15 years to about $355,000 in equity and generates increasing monthly cash flow.

When all components are combined after 15 years, the results are significantly stronger than focusing on any single strategy. The primary home builds substantial equity, the rental property adds another asset stream, investments grow to over $300,000, and reserves exceed $130,000. Altogether, the household reaches approximately $1.3 million in diversified wealth, along with multiple income streams and strong financial liquidity.

The key lesson is that integrated financial systems often outperform single-focus strategies. Instead of choosing between debt payoff, investing, or saving, this approach allows all three to grow together. The result is not just reduced debt—but a balanced, stable, and scalable path toward long-term financial independence.

Final Tips and Suggestions for Mortgage Freedom

The Complete Closing Guide to Building a Life Without Financial Pressure

Achieving mortgage freedom is not just a financial milestone—it is a transformation in how you think about money, time, and control over your life. For many people, the mortgage represents the largest and longest financial commitment they will ever make. Because of this, the journey toward paying it off or strategically eliminating it must be approached with clarity, patience, and structure. Mortgage freedom is not about rushing a single payoff event. It is about designing a financial system that gradually reduces dependency on debt while increasing income, assets, and flexibility.

One of the most important final lessons in this entire series is understanding that mortgage freedom does not always mean the mortgage is completely gone. For some people, freedom comes from eliminating the mortgage entirely. For others, it comes from having the mortgage fully covered by passive income. For others still, it comes from having enough investments, liquidity, and cash flow that the mortgage is no longer a source of stress or limitation. The definition of freedom is personal, but the principles used to achieve it remain consistent: discipline, structure, cash flow, and long-term thinking.

A key final strategy is learning how to reduce financial friction in your life. Financial friction refers to any unnecessary cost, inefficiency, or debt structure that slows down progress toward your goals. High-interest debt, lifestyle inflation, unused equity, and poor cash flow management all create friction. Reducing friction does not require extreme sacrifice. Instead, it requires awareness and intentional decision-making. Small improvements in spending habits, refinancing decisions, investment allocation, and cash flow management can significantly accelerate long-term mortgage payoff outcomes.

Another essential tip is to always treat your financial system as a long-term machine rather than a short-term reaction plan. Many people approach mortgage payoff emotionally, making decisions based on stress or excitement. They may aggressively pay down debt for a few months, then stop completely. They may invest heavily during good market conditions and retreat during uncertainty. This inconsistency slows down long-term progress. Mortgage freedom is built through systems, not emotions. Systems ensure that even when motivation fluctuates, progress continues. Consistency in cash flow allocation is one of the most powerful habits you can build. Whether you are paying extra toward your mortgage, investing in rental properties, or building reserves, consistency matters more than intensity. A steady $500 or $1,000 monthly contribution applied over many years often produces far greater results than sporadic large payments followed by long gaps of inactivity. Wealth is built through rhythm, not randomness.

Another important suggestion is to maintain strong financial reserves at all times. One of the most common mistakes people make is becoming overly aggressive with mortgage payoff while ignoring liquidity. While reducing debt is important, financial stability requires accessible cash. Emergencies, repairs, job changes, medical events, and investment opportunities all require liquidity. A well-prepared financial system always balances debt reduction with cash availability. Without reserves, even a low mortgage balance can become stressful during unexpected events.

It is also critical to avoid comparing your financial journey to others. Mortgage freedom is highly personal, and timelines vary widely depending on income, expenses, family structure, risk tolerance, and investment strategy. Some individuals may reach mortgage freedom in under ten years through aggressive payments and high income. Others may take twenty to thirty years while building investment portfolios alongside their mortgage. Both paths can lead to strong financial outcomes if managed correctly. Comparison often leads to unnecessary pressure and poor decision-making. Focus instead on consistency and progress relative to your own plan.

A powerful long-term suggestion is to use income increases strategically rather than lifestyle expansion. As income grows over time through promotions, business growth, or investment returns, many people naturally increase their spending. This is known as lifestyle inflation. While some lifestyle improvement is natural and healthy, excessive inflation can significantly slow mortgage payoff and wealth accumulation. A more effective strategy is to allocate a portion of every income increase toward mortgage reduction, investments, and reserves before expanding spending.

Refinancing can also play an important role in mortgage freedom when used correctly. Lower interest rates, shorter loan terms, or strategic restructuring may reduce total interest paid and accelerate payoff timelines. However, refinancing should always be evaluated carefully. Extending loan terms unnecessarily or repeatedly resetting amortization schedules can slow long-term progress. The goal is not just lower monthly payments but improved total financial positioning.

One of the most powerful final strategies is integrating multiple financial approaches rather than relying on a single method. Mortgage freedom is rarely achieved through one strategy alone. Instead, it is often the result of combining extra payments, rental income, refinancing, cash flow management, and disciplined saving. When multiple strategies work together, progress accelerates significantly. For example, rental income can be used to make extra mortgage payments while reserves protect against financial risk and investments grow in parallel.

Time remains one of the most important factors in achieving mortgage freedom. Many people underestimate how powerful long-term consistency becomes when combined with compounding. Even modest monthly efforts, when sustained over 10, 15, or 20 years, can produce dramatic reductions in debt and significant increases in net worth. The earlier you begin, the more time compounding has to work in your favor. However, it is never too late to begin improving your financial structure. Even small adjustments made today can create meaningful long-term impact.

Another important principle is maintaining flexibility. Financial plans should not be rigid. Life circumstances change. Income fluctuates. Markets shift. Family needs evolve. A strong mortgage freedom strategy is adaptable. It allows for adjustments without collapsing the entire system. Flexibility ensures that you can respond to opportunities or challenges without losing long-term direction. Risk awareness is also essential in the final stages of financial planning. As you build wealth, protect it. Insurance, reserves, diversified income streams, and conservative debt management become increasingly important. Wealth that is built without protection can be lost quickly. Wealth that is protected can last for generations. Mortgage freedom is not just about elimination of debt; it is about preservation of financial stability.

Emotional discipline is another critical factor. The final stage of mortgage freedom often requires resisting temptation. When equity grows, it can feel tempting to withdraw large amounts for lifestyle upgrades. When investments perform well, it can feel tempting to overextend. Emotional discipline ensures that financial decisions remain aligned with long-term goals rather than short-term desires. The ability to delay gratification is often what separates successful long-term wealth builders from those who plateau financially.

It is also important to recognize that mortgage freedom does not require perfection. Many people believe they must make flawless decisions or follow a perfect plan. In reality, wealth is built through consistent good decisions, not perfect ones. Mistakes may occur, markets may change, and unexpected events may arise. What matters most is maintaining direction over time rather than perfection in every moment. Another powerful suggestion is to regularly review and adjust your financial plan. Annual or semi-annual reviews help ensure that your mortgage strategy, investment approach, and cash flow management remain aligned with your goals. As income increases or expenses change, your allocation strategy may need to be updated. Financial planning is not a one-time event—it is an ongoing process.

Ultimately, mortgage freedom is about creating a life where financial obligations no longer control your decisions. Whether your mortgage is fully paid off, significantly reduced, or fully covered by investment income, the true goal is freedom of choice. It is the ability to live without financial pressure dictating your career, lifestyle, or future decisions.

The most successful individuals in this journey are those who think long term, act consistently, and balance multiple financial priorities at once. They do not rely on shortcuts or emotional decisions. Instead, they build systems that quietly and steadily move them toward freedom over time.

As you conclude this series, remember that mortgage freedom is not a single event—it is a process. It is built step by step, decision by decision, year by year. Every extra payment, every investment, every saved dollar, and every disciplined choice contributes to the final outcome.

If you remain consistent, patient, and strategic, mortgage freedom is not only possible—it becomes highly achievable. And once achieved, it opens the door to something far greater than financial security: it opens the door to complete control over your time, your future, and your life.

Real Life Final Example – The 20-Year Mortgage Freedom System

They didn't begin this plan by focusing only on "how fast can we pay off the mortgage." Instead, they started with a broader question: *"How do we structure $2,500 of monthly extra income so it builds multiple layers of wealth at the same time?"* With a $500,000 home, a $350,000 mortgage at 5.25%, and a manageable $2,170 monthly payment, they already had stability—the opportunity was how to turn surplus income into a long-term financial engine.

From the beginning, they committed to a disciplined allocation system rather than a single-purpose strategy. Every month, $1,000 was directed toward extra mortgage payments, $1,000 was invested into rental property growth, and $500 was set aside for emergency reserves. This structure ensured that debt reduction, investing, and financial protection were all happening simultaneously instead of competing against each other.

Over time, the mortgage strategy alone created a powerful impact. By consistently applying an additional $1,000 per month toward principal over 20 years, they contributed about $240,000 in extra payments. This reduced the mortgage timeline by approximately 15 years and saved an estimated $150,000 or more in interest. What would have been a 30-year obligation became a much shorter financial commitment, significantly reducing long-term pressure.

However, the real transformation came from what happened outside the mortgage. After about three years of consistent saving, the investor used accumulated funds to purchase a rental property for $320,000 with a $64,000 down payment. In the early years, it generated modest cash flow of $250 to $400 per month, but over time it grew into a much stronger asset. After 20 years, this property appreciated to approximately $640,000 in value, with about $460,000 in equity and around $1,200 per month in rental income.

At the same time, the investment and reserve strategies were compounding in the background. The $1,000 monthly investment account, growing at an average of 7%, expanded to approximately $490,000 over 20 years. The $500 monthly reserve allocation, growing at a more conservative 5%, built an additional $200,000+ safety cushion. Together, these accounts provided both growth and stability, ensuring the household was never financially overexposed. By the end of 20 years, the combined financial picture looked very different from a simple mortgage payoff strategy. The primary home had significant equity, the rental property had grown into a major income-producing asset, investments had nearly reached half a million dollars, and reserves provided strong liquidity protection. Altogether, total net assets exceeded approximately $1.65 million, along with ongoing passive income and reduced financial stress.

The key lesson is that wealth is rarely built from one decision alone. It is the result of systems working together over time—debt reduction reducing financial burden, investments compounding in thc background, real estate generating income and appreciation, and reserves protecting against uncertainty. When all four elements are aligned and executed consistently, financial independence becomes not just a goal, but a highly achievable outcome over time.

reserve allocation, growing at a more conservative 5%, built an additional $200,000 safety cushion. Together, these accounts provided both growth and stability, ensuring the household was never financially overexposed. By the end of 30 years, the combined financial picture looked very different from a simple mortgage payoff strategy. The primary home had significant equity, the rental property had grown into a major income-producing asset, investments had nearly reached half a million dollars, and reserves provided strong liquidity protection. Altogether, total net assets exceeded approximately $1.[illegible] million, along with ongoing passive income and reduced financial stress.

The key lesson is that wealth is rarely built from one decision alone. It is the result of systems working together over time—debt reduction reducing financial burden, investments compounding in the background, real estate generating income and appreciation, and reserves protecting against uncertainty. When all four elements are aligned and executed consistently, financial independence becomes not just a goal, but a highly achievable outcome over time.

www.ingramcontent.com/pod-product-compliance
Lightning Source LLC
LaVergne TN
LVHW040519210926
848480LV00007BA/1522
* 9 7 9 8 2 5 6 0 0 7 6 9 0 *